*& Further
Techniques for
Personal Growth
by
Muriel
Schiffman*

D1246208

GESTALT SELF THERAPY

Wingbow Press books are published and distributed by Bookpeople, 7900 Edgewater Drive, Oakland, California 94621.

Library of Congress Catalog Card Number 73-75228.
ISBN 0-914728-12-1.

Illustrated by Jessica Wilhelm.
Cover design by Michael Patrick Cronan.
Originally published by Self Therapy Press.

First Wingbow Press printing, October 1980
Second printing, September 1982
Third printing, January 1985
Fourth printing, October 1987
Fifth printing, September 1990
Sixth printing, October 1992

To Ann and Jean

with apologies

ACKNOWLEDGMENTS

I WANT to thank the following people: Lucy Stein for her unflagging devotion to my students; Hilda Flemming for her enthusiastic interest in my ideas and her conviction that they were worth writing about; my husband, Bernard Schiffman, for his patience and faith as well as for his practical help in preparing this manuscript. I am grateful to workshop members for teaching me more than I ever learned from books and helping me to grow.

Menlo Park, California
March 1971

CONTENTS

PREFACE

THIS BOOK can be used by readers without any background in psychology. However, it is an outgrowth of *SELF THERAPY Techniques for Personal Growth* and a condensation of that book is given in Appendix I.

TERMS USED IN THIS BOOK

Parent, Child and *Adult* within you. These are *not* used in exactly the same way as meant by Eric Berne [5] in transactional analysis. *Parent*: part of you that functions like a caricature, an exaggeration of authority figures from childhood; punishing scolding, judgmental. *Child*: hidden part that can feel old and forbidden emotions from the past. *Adult*: rational part, aware of present reality. The phrase "part of" does not imply that you are split into different parts, only that you function from time to time on different levels.

Acting out: Self-defeating behavior motivated by irrational, hidden feelings.

Projecting: Imagining that someone else is experiencing an emotion you yourself feel or are hiding from yourself.

Transference: Irrational attitude toward another whose behavior you distort in accordance with your own unresolved problems.

Hidden feelings: Unconscious emotions outside of awareness and conscious experience.

Resistance: Hidden fear of change, urge to maintain old defenses. The part of you that fights your efforts to grow, that sabotages psychotherapy.

1. DR. JEKYLL & MR. HYDE

I RECENTLY read "Dr. Jekyll and Mr. Hyde" [1] and realized how Hollywood sloughed over Robert Louis Stevenson's real message. Here is the tragedy of a man who deliberately separated the two sides of his nature, good and bad, "spiritual" and "bestial." The narrator says, "I learned to recognize the thorough and primitive duality of man; I saw that, of the two natures that contended in the field of my consciousness, even if I could rightly be said to be either, it was only because I was radically both; and . . . I had learned to dwell with pleasure, as a beloved daydream, on the thought of the *separation of these elements* (my italics). If each, I told myself, could be housed in separate identities, life would be relieved of all that was unbearable; the unjust might go his way, delivered from the aspirations and remorse of his upright twin; and the just could walk steadfastly and securely on his upward path, doing the good things in which he found his pleasure, and no longer exposed to disgrace and penitence by the hands of this extraneous evil. It was the curse of mankind that these incongruous faggots were thus bound together—that in the agonised womb of consciousness, these polar twins should be continuously struggling. How, then, were they dissociated?"

Dr. Jekyll found a chemical means of dissociating, of separating his two natures, and for a while his "beloved daydream" was fulfilled. But gradually his bad side became stronger, uncontrollable and murderous. Dr. Jekyll grew so frightened and horrified at Mr. Hyde's brutal acts that he tried to stop the process, determined never to step into that role again. But it was too late. His bad side, separated too long from his good side, was now so powerful that he no longer had control over it. At unexpected moments, involuntarily, Dr. Jekyll began to find himself changing into the person he now loathed and feared, the bestial Mr. Hyde.

I felt a shock of recognition when I read this story.

There, but for the grace of God, go I. I too had tried to separate the two sides of myself. I too had carefully hidden the part of me that is cruel and angry like the people who degraded me in childhood, had deliberately played the role of Dr. Jekyll, gentle, saintly, all-loving. And sometimes, with my small children, Mr. Hyde took over: I scolded, nagged, manipulated just like S., my stepmother. Without self therapy I might have succeeded in further separating those two sides of myself. I might eventually have acted out the degrading and brutalizing part of me that is like Mrs. L., my earlier, sadistic foster mother.

I see Dr. Jekyll-Mr. Hyde tragedies among my students. Here are some examples. Ben lives on that see-saw. He has so successfully separated the two parts of his personality that those who know only the warm, affectionate Dr. Jekyll are dumfounded and shaken when they first experience him as Mr. Hyde, degrading and frightening.

Alcohol, like Dr. Jekyll's miraculous chemical, can change some people into the hidden, Mr. Hyde side of their personalities. When Beth was a little girl she literally thought she had two mothers. The sober mother was loving and gentle. The drunken mother was so repulsive and terrifying that little Beth used to cry for her "other" mother to come back.

Some people are so successful in separating the two sides of themselves that they literally drive themselves crazy. Leo refuses to experience anger in any form and has turned himself into a statue of a saint, cool, rigid, unspontaneous. He has dissociated himself from his angry side so effectively that this part of him can only come alive with occasional spurts of destructive rage in psychotic breaks.

Selma distrusted the soft, warm side of her nature. She deliberately cultivated a tough, cold personality to ward off feelings of helplessness and hurt. As time went on she discovered that the mask of hardness was taking over against her will. At moments when she desperately longed to let herself go, to feel and express tenderness, she was frozen in that hard armor, alienated from other people and from the warmth of her own humanity. Only the long, painful work of self therapy freed her softer self from that imprisonment in the jail of her own making.

My purpose here is to teach you how to integrate the opposite sides of yourself.

2. THE INNER CONFLICT

THIS BOOK grew out of my traumatic and therapeutic experience with Dr. Frederick (Fritz) Perls, father of gestalt
therapy. To those who knew Fritz, the phrase "traumatic
and therapeutic" is not a contradiction. He believed the
therapist's task is to frustrate the patient to the point of
desperation, the therapeutic impasse. At that point he
may have the courage to thrash about, flounder until he
finds a new way for himself.

Years ago I went to Esalen Institute at Big Sur to join
Fritz' five-day gestalt workshop. I went in fear and trembling, having heard terrifying tales about the charismatic
personality of this man. My catastrophic expectations, to
use Fritz' phrase, were amply fulfilled. That was in the
bad, old days before he had mellowed to the gentleness of
his later years. At the end of that workshop, even Fritz
admitted he had gone too far, been too cruel.

Like many neurotics, I formed an instant transference on
Fritz; he was a father figure to me. I longed desperately
for his love which he consistently withheld. All week I used
my own self therapy techniques (Appendix I) just to survive.
I could neither eat nor sleep: I just worked. Time and
again, peeling away layers of my feelings toward Fritz, I
discovered more and more hidden feelings about my own
father.

As a result of that intensive work, I took a giant step
forward in my personal growth. But I dared not return to
another of his gestalt workshops until three years later.

I worked in self therapy on my transference and finally
reached a point where I no longer needed his love, no longer
needed to be Daddy's favorite child. Now I could feel like a
student; I was ready to learn. In my second gestalt workshop I told Fritz about the new place I was in. "I want to
learn," I said. "Teach me." So from time to time, Fritz
very graciously shared his thinking with me.

4

THE INNER CONFLICT

"I am working now entirely on bringing the unconscious fantasies into consciousness. Everything is projection," he pronounced.

Everything? That seemed a pretty broad statement. I could not swallow it. (Projection means you imagine the other person is feeling an emotion that is really your own.) Yes, I could see that much of our distortion was projection, but surely not *everything*! Often, it seemed to me, we imagine others are acting toward us as people did in our past, but this did not necessarily mean that we ourselves were acting that way.

In the year between my second and third workshop with Fritz, I did a little gestalt self therapy, mostly with dreams. But in the main I relied on my old self therapy techniques. I gave some gestalt self therapy lectures. A few times, working with students who were too far away from their apparent feelings to use my old self therapy methods, I taught them Fritz's use of dreams.

During my third gestalt workshop, I realized I still had a transference on Fritz: his approval and fantasized disapproval were still too important. During the following months in self therapy I discovered other people, both male and female, besides my father, whom Fritz represented to me. Some time during that year I became free to use what I learned from him.

I began to do gestalt self therapy more frequently. When a book on Fritz's workshops [3] appeared I gobbled it up. My mother's recent death had plunged me into old conflicts. This book was a shot in the arm for me. All my experiences and observations in those three gestalt workshops, the intervening years of self therapy about Fritz, began to fit into place.

I began a regular weekly regime for myself of gestalt self therapy sessions (in addition to my old self therapy techniques applied to any inappropriate emotion that cropped up in between). Unlike my other techniques, gestalt self therapy can be scheduled: you can start in cold blood, you do not need to wait to feel an apparent emotion hot off the griddle.

In a little while I began to see the startling truth in

5

Fritz's seemingly arbitrary statement, "Everything is projection." My whole attitude toward the problem of inner growth changed. It was like shifting gears. My lectures changed radically. I was no longer satisfied to see my students coast along, using self therapy merely to relieve discomfort, to live more easily with daily problems. I saw that some of them were using my methods as crutches to hobble along. I wanted to tell them they could walk like free men if they would only dare first to creep on their bellies for a little while like infants, feel their helplessness for brief moments.

I began to sound like an evangelist preacher, pleading with my students to raise their eyes to a higher goal, to seek genuine growth instead of mere adjustment to their neuroses. Little by little I learned, from verbal and non-verbal feedback, that many of them could not understand me.

What did I want to tell them? Something like this: My first book [4] taught people how to avoid acting out their neurotic tendencies. By peeling away skins of the onion that is my whole complicated personality (layer upon layer of pseudo-emotions and attitudes accumulated through the years), I can reach the true feelings underneath. We had learned, my students and I, that sometimes the apparent emotion directed toward a present day person or event was a disguise covering a reaction toward something from the past. Irrationally furious with your spouse for no good reason? Self therapy may bring you back to an emotion you avoided feeling long ago toward a parent; then the apparent emotion toward your husband or wife evaporates, you are rational again. [See Appendix I]

This is a good system for getting along day by day. You learn to recognize and cope with your neurotic distortions of reality; little by little, daring to feel your true emotions, you can avoid much of your self defeating behavior, accumulate more satisfying experiences and grow healthier.

Through the years of observing people through letters, conferences, and workshops, I began to notice that some of them were using self therapy techniques but not really changing. They had developed a technique which brought relief from intense, painful emotions; they were suffering

6

fewer periods of anxiety and depression; they were "handling" others, from time to time, with more finesse. But the basic neurosis, the warped view of life, of themselves and others, remained intact. Periodically they reverted to their old self defeating patterns completely unchanged, picking up the pieces after each fiasco with an attitude of "Oops! I slipped. Sorry about that," going back to what looked like learned "good" behavior without any real self awareness.

I began to see what they were doing with self therapy. They were going back to the past for three reasons:

1) to get relief from present painful emotions;
2) to justify apparent emotions ("No wonder I hate my wife! She's just like my mother.")
3) to learn new ways of handling people to get what they thought they needed.

My self therapy techniques were designed for personal growth. Some students, like myself, are using them:

1) to become more truly self aware, to assume more responsibility for their lives instead of blaming others;
2) to accumulate good experiences in daily life which strengthen them so they can work toward the further goal of becoming more like the kind of people they want to be.

But others are using self therapy simply to adjust, to get along with their old neuroses more comfortably. These have the fantasy that they have no inner resources, that everything they need comes from other people: respect, recognition, approval, love. They have two main goals in therapy:

1) to avoid pain;
2) to learn better ways to get what they think they need from the world.

This kind of adjustment therapy is not good enough for me and I do not want to teach it. I realized many of my students needed a new orientation. I had to show them a higher goal, a dream of self fulfillment, of real growth.

"Everything is projection." Over and over again I explained that when you use self therapy to explore a hidden feeling about someone else, when you discover he reminds you of someone from the past, you *must not stop working.* Go further. Whenever you over-react to someone or something in the present because of someone in your past, it means you have swallowed down that person (father, mother, sibling). He is an undigested lump in you; you must experience him as part of yourself. It is not enough to blame your father for hurting you. You yourself are now hurting, or would like to hurt someone in the same way.

Each person from the past with whom we have unfinished business, toward whom we dared not experience and act on our true feelings, lives within us and directs some area of our lives. In order to grow and be our true selves, we must go back to those unfinished situations, feel the old forbidden emotions and experience those hidden parts of ourselves that are just like the people who once frustrated us. This is the real work of therapy; if we do it often enough we can chew up those undigested lumps of people, integrate some parts of them into ourselves and spit up what we cannot use.

Gestalt therapy is a tool designed for that hard, essential work. I began to teach it in all my lectures and I could see in a little while that some students were ready for it but many were not. I could tell from oral and written feedback that the second group wanted more and better techniques for feeling comfortable and for handling other people. My frustration about this pushed me into doing more gestalt self therapy: I explored my obsession with communication from many angles. Then I began to remember letters from strangers who had read my book, SELF THERAPY, people who were so ready for self therapy that they could learn without any personal contact with me. My missionary zeal burned: I wanted desperately to reach people somewhere who were ready to face themselves squarely, who wanted to change, who were no longer satisfied to limp along and adjust to their neuroses. I decided to stop lecturing for a while and write another book.

Gestalt therapy, like psychodrama, is a way of consciously enacting, in concrete form, your unconscious fantasies. When you work with a therapist or gestalt group leader, he can guide you, give you a push in the direction of solving a neurotic problem. In gestalt *self* therapy you are on your own. The purpose, as with any kind of self therapy, is to *know where you are*.

I want to *know myself*; to be truly aware of the opposing forces within me; to consciously experience the battle raging beneath the surface, that battle whose distant thunder I tend to smother with clenched teeth, headaches, obsessive thinking. When I get down there and plunge into the battle scene, I can experience what Fritz calls the "therapeutic impasse."

Webster defines impasse as "an impassable road or way; a predicament affording no obvious escape." When I try to solve a problem and discover how useless my old neurotic ways are, when I let myself feel the frustration and helplessness, thrashing about desperately for a way out, I am experiencing the therapeutic impasse. Only then, only by hitting rock bottom, do I have a chance to strike out on a new path.

Any time you over-react to another person, no matter how "real" his behavior appears to be, you are projecting something on to him. This is the time to use gestalt self therapy to discover something about the hidden side of yourself. As in any kind of self therapy, once you experience the hidden feeling, the apparent feeling with which you began evaporates. You may come out of self therapy still disliking the person but the rage or fear or depression is gone.

Nobody ever got better in the psychiatrist's office. Self therapy, self awareness, "insights" alone are not enough to change you; nor can pure "will power" (the Parent using brute force to break the Child's spirit) do the trick. Real growth comes as a result of *self awareness* plus *experiments in new behavior*, as described in the chapter, "Self Discipline."

Each time I live through the inner struggle I recognize the terrible chasm between the two sides of myself. After each gestalt experience I find some small area of choice, a compromise between those two opposing forces. Little by little, working over and over again on the same dichotomy, I see the gap narrowing, the difficulty of making choices less desperate. My goal is to integrate the two opposite sides of myself, to end the inner battle.

Little by little I can see myself getting nearer that goal. When I experience the two conflicting sides in gestalt self therapy, each side appears to be extreme and irrational. I cannot guess what I will be like when the work is done, what the middle way will be, the medium between these two extremes. Harry Stack Sullivan said each of us is a mere caricature of what he might be. I long to know what my true self will be when these distortions are gone.

What is the difference between a) the psychology of adjustment and b) gestalt therapy? In a) the psychology of adjustment your goals are narrow. You want to get along a little more comfortably with your neurosis. You are afraid of any real change. In b) gestalt therapy you are truly growth oriented. You want to know who you really are, to discard the old threadbare cloak of defenses even if it means feeling naked for a while. If you are merely interested in adjustment, you are terrified of nakedness and you hang on to that inadequate cloak for dear life. To you, any present pain is preferable to the unknown.

The person committed to adjustment has two main goals:

1. To control others. He lives out the fantasy that all his sources of life, fulfillment, joy come from other people and/or things. He uses therapy to modify his self-defeating behavior so as to become more proficient at *getting*.

The tragedy is he stops himself from true growth; he never taps his own inner resources so he never learns that the sources of life, fulfillment and joy are within himself. Furthermore, because he is afraid of any real inner change, the modification of his behavior can only be temporary, spasmodic, since it is superficial. It works for a while: he seems to be more adept at "handling" people and events, but periodically pressure builds up from the constant battle he is trying to ignore. Suddenly—bang! He is acting out some irrational, self-defeating pattern and down comes the house of cards he so painstakingly built. Then he has to begin "learning" all over again how to "behave." His life is a series of periods of reform and rebellion.

2. The other goal of the adjustment man is to bolster up his self esteem. He tries to collect experiences, thoughts,

THE INNER CONFLICT

feelings which will ward off his basic conviction of worthlessness. This is self-defeating in two ways: a) When he has been on his good behavior for a while, using his new knowledge to "get along" better, to manipulate people and events successfully, he begins to project the Parent in his head on to others. He fantasies that they are forcing him to behave himself. The rebellious Adolescent in him now begins to rage. He feels degraded, outraged by his own careful, conforming, appeasing behavior. His self esteem falls rapidly and in order to bolster it he erupts into impulsive behavior. He "proves" to the people around him that he is not afraid of them. This is when the house of cards collapses.

If he would look within at such times and experience the inner battle, he would not have to act out his unconscious fantasy of the scolded child surrounded by Parents. He would not be compelled to rebel against them in order to bolster up his self esteem.

But the adjustment man is so preoccupied with the task of making himself "feel better," warding off pain, that he would rather blame others than go into his own feelings. It's easier to pass the buck than to assume responsibility for his own misery, easier to "escape into reality," to fight with others, than to experience the inner struggle.

In order to do gestalt therapy, to be truly growth oriented, you must be able to experience both *self hatred* and *hope.* One without the other is not enough.

Self hatred feels like shame, guilt, helplessness. You are scolding yourself for being bad, stupid or neurotic. Sometimes you *obey* that scolding voice instead of simply *listening* to it. When you obey it, you function as a frightened, appeasing child, cowering in a corner. "Yes, I know I'm bad, stupid, sick. Hit me again. I deserve this punishment."

You are trying to appease the Parent in your head instead of confronting him. You are manipulating him the way you manipulate others. "If I can make him feel sorry for me, he'll stop punishing me." This is a way of avoiding the real work of therapy which is to experience two opposite sides of yourself in a real dialogue.

You get temporary relief with that kind of self therapy, appeasing the Parent, just as you do when crying at a movie. But at the movie, unless you ask yourself, "What does this remind me of? What am I *really* crying about?", [4] you are not helping yourself to change. When you stay with the self hatred, avoiding a confrontation with the scolding Parent, you are not growing. Whenever you appease a tyrant or a bully, the relief can only be temporary.

The truth is, if you were *all* bad, stupid or sick, you wouldn't be scolding yourself. The scolding itself proves you have certain standards for yourself, that there is a part of you that wants to be better. When you ignore that part, when you succumb to unadulterated self-blame, you are being phony and cowardly. You are welcoming punishment, the punishment of depression, for example, instead of facing the inner conflict that might give you courage to change. You are taking the easy way out, getting some quick, temporary relief. You can get quick, temporary relief from a lump in your throat when you cry at a movie, but unless you go into your hidden feelings nothing new can happen to you.

The *hope* for change gives us the courage to do the real work of therapy, to confront the scolding Parent instead of agreeing with it in a hurry so it will shut up. The person succumbing to self hatred in order to get temporary relief sounds like this, "I'm so worthless, I don't deserve to live. I ought to kill myself. Why can't I do right? I'm just so bad, stupid, sick, I feel like giving up. I'd like to kill myself but I'm too cowardly to do that," etc. until he can work up to a good cry; then he feels better for a while. The Parent in his head stops punishing for a while, just as a real parent says to a sobbing child, "Well, as long as you admit you're a bad boy, and I see you are truly sorry, then I don't need to punish you any more, until next time." And next time always comes.

Only by experiencing the *two* sides of yourself, recognizing the gap between them, is there a chance for the gap to narrow, for the two opposites to grow less extreme, closer to one another. Each time you experience the inner struggle, the Adult part of you becomes a little stronger. You are free to make some small choice, perform some real action, to disprove the Parent's verdict, to strengthen the opposition, to improve your self image.

But each time you merely succumb to the Parent (act out the weak, beaten Child) the Adult weakens, is less able to protect the Child. This failure to change behavior further strengthens the Parent, justifies the punishment. The gap between the opposite sides grows wider, the battle fiercer.

The trouble with neurotic patterns is that they are not static. If we don't get better, we won't stand still. We get worse.

The growth oriented person needs to feel both hope and self hatred. What about hope alone?

If you hope to change but dare not allow yourself to experience self hatred, constantly warding off guilt, shame, helplessness, you are avoiding the inner conflict. This system can become a form of self hypnosis ("I can get better, I will become healthier") where you build up more and more defenses, get further away from your real feelings. The inner battle rages on unseen until it has to burst out in a spell of anxiety, depression, physical illness, etc.

Each of us lives in a waking dream based on the past. The neurotic (and the so-called "normal" person—one with mildly neurotic tendencies) rarely experiences the here-and-now. He distorts present people and events to fit his bad dream. Perls calls the dream the "unconscious fantasy"; Eric Berne [5] refers to the "script," the hidden blueprint a person follows to make his future like his past. We distort new people and events and fit them into the same old boxes, providing ourselves with the same old frustrating experiences. Angyal [6] talks about the neurotic's "private mythology," his inner convictions and prejudices which help him misinterpret reality. In my work, I see how desperately people fight to hang on to their misconceptions, how carefully they screen out and distort experiences which might contradict their theories about life. In order to justify their feelings of distrust, fear, helplessness, rage, they shut their eyes and close their ears saying, in effect, "Don't confuse me with facts."

If I am living in my waking dream, I cannot see you clearly. And if I bump into you at a time when you are caught up in *your* dream, you have to distort me too. I have described elsewhere [4] what happens when two people are being irrational at the same time, when their interaction involves an area where both are distorting. Whenever we function on this dream level, we are hiding some feeling from ourselves. That hidden emotion belongs to an earlier, more primitive way of reasoning, incompatible with our adult thinking.

There are two important factors here:

1. It is hard for the adult intellect to understand that anachronistic way of reasoning. This is one reason why self therapy is difficult. If someone told you that despite your apparent anger, you were really afraid of a little person, half your size and age, you would laugh. But to the child within you, that small figure, may loom large and threatening.

2. When you *do* get down to that hidden feeling, your adult self can deal more rationally with the problem. But, whenever you are hiding something from yourself, you use some fake feeling as a cover, so you act in a self defeating way. If it's love you want, you will get rejection. If you are seeking approval, you find disapproval. If you are trying to build up your self respect, you manage to make a fool of yourself.

Once you feel your hidden emotion, you no longer need the self defeating apparent emotion which covered it. It evaporates. Besides that, the Adult recognizes the inappropriateness of the hidden emotion and is not compelled to act it out. Having experienced the child within you, the part of you that has been maturing and learning all these years can make an adult decision.

We cannot know others when we do not know ourselves. Whenever we have difficulty seeing the world around us, we must look within to clear our outward vision.

Self awareness is preparation, not a substitute for self therapy. On occasion you recognize a self defeating pattern of behavior: you realize your apparent emotion is inappropriate. If, instead of using this clue for self therapy, you rely on your intellect to solve the problem, ignoring the hidden feelings, you will fail. If your baby is crying, you do not assume you can fulfill his need without first checking to see if he just finished a meal, is cold and wet, or has a pin sticking into him. Whenever you feel an inappropriate emotion, the Child within you is crying. You cannot make a wise decision unless you know what he is crying about.

When the sophisticated neurotic notices himself playing a game that feels intolerable to him, he exchanges it for another and pretends to himself that he is "getting better" [4]. He develops some self awareness, recognizes a self defeating pattern of behavior, and *without exploring the hidden reasons* for that behavior, sets out to change it.

The truth is he has noticed only *one* irrational side of himself in action. It seems to him that he is now thinking clearly, that he can make a rational decision. Since he is avoiding the inner conflict, he can only change sides, act out another equally irrational, self defeating tendency.

So long as you avoid experiencing both sides of the struggle, you see-saw back and forth, first acting out one side and then the other, and when you have manipulated people and events with one set of attitudes, the other side will take over and sabotage the first side's efforts. A clue to this switching of sides (which feels deceptively like growth) is making good resolutions with a certain amount of bravado. This means you are functioning, not on the Adult level, but merely obeying one voice, the scolding Parent (Shape up! Stop being so bad, stupid, crazy!), the helpless Child (I give up, I'm just too bad, stupid, crazy to hack it.), or the rebellious Adolescent (I'm sick of being good. I just want to have fun and feel strong.)

The Dr. Jekyll-Mr. Hyde switch sounds something like this:

"I will be strong. To hell with other people's opinion!" versus extreme fear of disapproval and punishment.

"I will not be appeasing. I will not degrade myself. I will be honest (punishing, judgmental, degrading)" versus appeasing, manipulating, blackmailing, self-degrading.

"I will not feel fear or helplessness" versus fear, anxiety, helplessness.

"I will be loving" versus alienation, coldness, boredom with others' suffering.

"I will be friendly" versus hostility and fear of others, alienation, loneliness.

"I will keep cool and rational" versus hysteria, exploitation of apparent emotions to manipulate others.

"I will be tactful, concerned with others' feelings" versus self-centeredness, alienation, boredom and lack of curiosity about others.

"I will stop teaching" versus need to handle others, avoid own feelings.

"I will stop begging for sympathy" versus obsessive self pity and craving for sympathy.

"I will stop manipulating" versus compulsion to manipulate.

"I will stop pretending" versus phoniness, fear of rejection of real self.

A person makes these good resolutions in order to find a more effective way to bolster up his self esteem. He wants to feel better right away, to avoid further pain. Unfortunately, this system never works. The relief is only temporary, and then he switches back to the other side. I am constantly amazed at the short-lived memory of the person who lives on this see-saw. Each time I hear him announcing a "new" way of life, with much fanfare and rejoicing in what he imagines is new-found freedom from neurosis, I distinctly remember the exact same words, with the exact same celebration, weeks, months, or years ago. It would appear that the wish to change, without undergoing the pain of inner confrontation, affects the intellectual processes so that an otherwise intelligent person is able to kid himself in this way.

Self awareness is *preliminary* to self therapy. Focusing on others avoids the work of therapy. As long as you stay with the apparent feeling and find ways to justify it, you are wasting opportunities for inner growth, digging yourself deeper into the quagmire of distorted perception.

THE INNER CONFLICT

Martin Buber [2] describes those who are capable of doing the real work of therapy and those who are not. He uses language different from mine, but he is basically discussing the problems covered in this chapter.

Buber defines the *good* man as one who is unified, not conflicted. The *wicked* man cannot make wise decisions because of his inner conflict. In effect, his behavior is self-defeating. There is hope for the wicked man however; he can work toward unification of his inner conflicts and become good.

The *sinful* man, in Buber's terms, is a more serious case for whom there is little hope. He is one who is not motivated to change. He glorifies his own wrong direction, saying, "That's the way I am. I am a law unto myself. If I do it, it's right."

We can redefine the wicked man as the neurotic who is aware of his self-defeating behavior and has an opportunity to do the work of gestalt self therapy, integrate the conflicting parts of his personality and grow into health. The sinful man is the person who does not want to change. He does not allow himself to experience the therapeutic self-hatred, the guilt and shame which motivate us to do the hard work of therapy. His own best audience, he is fascinated by his own irrational acting out and justifies it. His attitude toward his own neurotic behavior resembles that of an overly indulgent parent toward a spoiled child: "Look at that naughty boy! Isn't he cute?"

3. TECHNIQUES FOR GESTALT SELF THERAPY

GESTALT THERAPY is a little like psychodrama. In psychodrama, you and other people sometimes reenact actual scenes from your own real or fantasy life. Others take on roles with which you interact. In gestalt therapy, you yourself play all the roles. In psychodrama, other people play the different parts of your personality. In gestalt therapy you play all the parts yourself.

In gestalt *self* therapy you have no outside guidance. You do it all yourself; you are completely responsible for getting the most out of the experience.

In this chapter I will outline three different techniques for gestalt self therapy.

I. Exploring a *known fantasy*, one you have already discovered through 1) self-awareness, intellectual observation of irrational patterns of behavior, or 2) experiencing a hidden feeling in self therapy.

II. Playing all the parts of a recurrent or disturbing *dream*.

III. Playing an imaginary encounter with a *person* who has aroused an inappropriate reaction: irrational feeling, obsessive thinking, anxiety, depression, psychosomatic symptoms.

I. EXPLORING A KNOWN FANTASY

Many times in self therapy I have peeled away a layer of an apparent emotion and reached a certain hidden feeling that I knew was also irrational, yet I could not go any deeper. For example, whenever I was taken by surprise by something good coming my way, I would get depressed. Unexpected good luck in landing a job, my students chipping in to buy me a gift, Bernie's decision to buy a house more elegant than I expected, someone doing me an unexpected favor:

any of these could push me into a mild depression. At one time it would take weeks before I got around to doing self therapy. Nowadays I can feel sadness before depression sets in, and use it for self therapy. The hidden feeling always is, "I'm not supposed to have this good luck. Something's wrong. I am supposed to have bad luck. It was decided long ago that my fate was unhappiness. Somewhere along the line the cards got mixed up and I have somebody else's good luck. That means someone else has my bad luck and it's all wrong. Somebody else is suffering, while I enjoy his good luck, and so I must not enjoy it."

Each time I feel this hidden thing the apparent emotion, the depression or sadness, disappears and in a few minutes the hidden emotion evaporates, too.

One day I decided to try gestalt self therapy on this fantasy. I have described [4] self therapy techniques that cannot be used unless you are in the midst of an apparent emotion. Gestalt self therapy is different: you can start in cold blood and gradually work your way into the feelings. My way is to set up a specific date, usually once a week, to do gestalt self therapy. During the week I use my old self therapy techniques to explore any painful problem that crops up and I think about my gestalt assignment all week. I decide in advance which things I need to work on: uncomfortable situations nagging but not arousing a strong enough feeling for regular self therapy, obsessive thinking, or hidden feelings like this one which bring relief from the immediate apparent emotion but are obviously covers for something deeper. I use my intellect to plan an attack and to guess about the path I will take, so when I do gestalt I can plunge right into the dialogue without hesitation.

I expect it to sound and feel wooden at the start, and I always have a great reluctance to get into it. It always feels as if nothing real could possibly happen. But I doggedly plow my way through, saying the words in a matter-of-fact, emotionless way, not faking it, until it comes alive, and in a few minutes it always does. While I am speaking the lines I am also listening to them. As in my chapter, "Sneaking Up on the Unconscious" [4], while feeling a strong emotion I ask myself, "What does this remind me of?" "Who did this to whom?" Then I change one or both of the roles and continue with a similar dialogue.

I never forget that my purpose in gestalt self therapy is to experience hidden parts of myself. Whenever I hear myself speaking words that apply to some part of myself, I change roles and go on with the inner dialogue, the confrontation between two sides of me.

Here is a condensed version of what happened.

> Muriel: I know there was a mistake in the cards. I have to find that other person. How can I find him? (Here I began to cry and continued through most of the experience.) I'm eating up all the food and somewhere a starved person needs me. Where are you? I'm looking for you. Please tell me where you are.

> Starved Person: I'm starving. Muriel, where are you? I need you. Save me.

> Muriel: I can't find you. I want to feed you, but I can't find you.

> S.P.: Save me, feed me, I'm starving. Give me some, you have so much. (At this point I switched the dialogue to the two parts of myself.)

> Muriel 1: I want to save all those deprived people, but I can't. I don't know how.

> Muriel 2: You are a rotten, greedy thing. You have no right to all those good things. You have Bernie and work you enjoy, and children you're proud of, and your health. Shame on you for gobbling up all the good things in life.

> Muriel 1: I want to share, I want to give. What can I do?

> Muriel 2: (Screaming) I hate you, you selfish, greedy thing.

That was as far as I could get then.

The next time I worked on this fantasy, I put my body into it. I began by play-acting. Although I avoided any phoniness, by going through my lines without emotion, I stood up tall

20

with my arms outstretched in an attitude of saintly generosity, the all-giving mother, the Statue of Liberty.

Muriel: Come to me, poor starving people. I will feed you, I have so much and I want to give.

S.P.: You're a liar. You make promises you can't fulfill. (The whole thing came alive at this point.)

Muriel: (Crying) No, it's not true. I want to feed you.

S.P.: You keep promising, but I'm still starving, and you're gobbling up all the food, you greedy thing. I hate you.

Muriel: I want to, but I don't know how. I don't want all this food. I'm gagging on it. I'm satiated.
(Here the starving person became Little Muriel, the child I once was.)

Little Muriel: You promised me when you grew up I'd be happy. You lied. You failed me.

Muriel: I'm sorry. I want to rescue you, but I don't know how.

Little M: You've got everything now, and I'm still back here suffering. Save me, save me.

Muriel: I want to but I can't. I don't know how.

Little M: You promised. You lied to me. You failed me.

Muriel: Forgive me. I can't help it.

Little M: (Screams) Take care of me. Save me, save me.

Muriel: I can't, I can't.

Here I came out of the self therapy and realized I had been trying to be my own mother ever since she left me when I was five, and I could not do it any more. I felt I could not feed that emotionally starved Child. I understood now a recurrent dream: I am ready to serve a dinner party. The table is set, I open the oven and discover I have forgotten to buy the roast. I feel frantic with guilt and helplessness.

I also understood my recent aversion to my own food. For the past month I had only been able to enjoy restaurant meals. Nothing I prepared myself seemed appetizing. That food represented the good things in my life, my good luck which the Child within me, stuck in the past, envied and resented.

Another fantasy

I had known for some time that my compulsive overworking was irrational. It was hard to find time for recreation when unread students' mail and unfinished household chores loomed up. Often, when I was out to have a good time my mind was so cluttered up with students' problems, lectures, workshops, that I could not have fun. My stepmother was long dead, but I discovered in self therapy that I was still obeying her.

Muriel: I am so tired.

Stepmother: You're not working hard enough. Come on, stop fooling around. Do those chores, you lazy thing. Don't tell me you're tired. You're just lazy.

Muriel: Oh please, let me play.

S.M.: Play? What do you mean, play? You have all those things to do. Get to work.

Muriel: You never let me have any fun. I'm so tired of working all the time. I need some fun.

S.M.: All you care about is fun. Just like your mother. Irresponsible.

Muriel: Oh, no! Please don't tell me I'm like my mother. I don't desert my children.
(Here I switched to two sides of Muriel: Parent & Child)

Parent: Just like your mother, you big phoney. Pretending to love everybody. All you care about is a good time.

Child: It's not true. I do love them. I won't desert them. I just need a little time off.

22

Parent: I hate you, selfish thing. (pounding chair) Just like your mother.

Child: Stop torturing me. I'm doing the best I can. Let me rest.

Parent: I hate you, hate you.

Child: Please!

Now I understood another meaning of the dream of the missing roast: my fear of being a depriving mother.

When the gestalt self therapy experience is over, when my feelings have cooled off, my Adult self takes over. I ask myself, "What do I know about myself now? In terms of my inner conflicts, where am I at this point?" Then two things happen: a) the hidden fantasy has a little less power over my attitudes and behavior because I am more aware of it, I have less compulsion to act out self defeating patterns and b) the Adult finds some small area of choice, some decision which is a compromise between the two opposing forces.

I notice that with repeated gestalt experiences of the same conflicts over a period of time, my life style is altering. The gap between the two sides appears to be narrowing. My goal is to close the gap, to integrate those two opposites so that the inner struggle stops completely and I can function in each of these conflicted areas like Maslow's healthy person[9]: spontaneous, non-blocked, unconflicted.

II. DREAMS

Fritz believed that modern man is so intellect-oriented, so lacking in spontaneity, that only in dreams can he be truly genuine. On the other hand, Harry Stack Sullivan said that by the time we start remembering our dreams we have already distorted them. Research indicates that patients obligingly produce Freudian dreams, Jungian dreams, Adlerian dreams, etc. to fit the theories of their therapists.

My own observation is that people who get too absorbed in analyzing their dreams tend to ignore their responsibilities in daily life. In general, I am against contemplating one's navel at the expense of real self awareness. Most of us need

23

encouragement to notice our self defeating behavior in everyday life, to explore our mistakes in problem solving, in our relations with other people, rather than escaping into preoccupation with dreams.

But there are two kinds of dreams I find worth working with: 1) a recurrent dream and 2) a dream that stays with you the next day, producing depression, anxiety or obsessive thinking.

Every part of the dream is yourself. Play each role: people and things. Remember the purpose of gestalt self therapy is to experience all parts of yourself, especially the hidden parts. When you are playing the dream and have felt some emotions as deeply as possible, when they have reached a peak and are beginning to cool off, just *before* they disappear, ask yourself, "What does this remind me of?" and change the characters in the dream to parts of yourself.

The Dream

I suddenly remember that I have forgotten to feed and water some white rats in the basement, for whom I am responsible. Filled with fear and remorse, I rush downstairs and find the rats stretched out on the floor, feebly trying to reach a puddle of water nearby. I am overwhelmed with pity and revulsion. I want them to reach the water but can't bear to touch them.

Rat: (Lying on floor) Muriel, save me. I'm dying. (Stretching arms toward water.) I can't reach the water.

Muriel: (Crying) Oh, poor little thing. I want to save you but I can't.

Rat: Please, please help me.

Muriel: Try harder, I can't touch you. You're so repulsive. I'm sorry.

Rat: I'm too weak. I can't. Muriel, help me, give me water.

Muriel: You're so pitiful but you make my flesh crawl.

Rat: (Getting weaker) Dying, dying.
(At this point, I suddenly saw the rat as part of me.)

Muriel 1: I know who you are. You're the part that's greedy for success. I hate you. You're disgusting.

Muriel 2: I need, I need, give me. Don't let me die.

Muriel 1: You're insatiable, I'm tired of feeding you. Stop blaming me.

Muriel 2: Give me, give me.

Muriel 1: Repulsive little thing, I know you. Whenever I accomplish anything real, help anyone grow, there you are, gloating about your *success*, as if that matters. I can't stand you. I hate you.

Muriel 2: Help, help, please.

Muriel 1: Sick of you. I want to rest. Can't feed you any more.

Muriel 2: (feebly gasps) I'm dying.

Muriel 1: THEN DIE, damn you. (stamps on Muriel 2)

Muriel 2: (Dies)

I was outgrowing an old trait I had long been ashamed of, and had done self therapy about in past years: the craving for recognition, status, prestige in my work. I don't know when the change occurred because I had not been paying attention to it recently, but after this gestalt self therapy experience, I began to notice that I was no longer excited by praise and signs of acceptance from the establishment; it was pleasant, but not thrilling. I realized that at last I was in a place I had wanted to be: that the fascination of my work and my feelings about my students were sufficient incentives for learning and working harder. Popularity, and acceptance by the establishment, no longer preoccupied me.

25

GESTALT SELF THERAPY

The Dream

I suddenly remember that I am responsible for a baby and have forgotten all about it. I know the baby has milk, but it is probably very wet and should have been fed additional nourishing foods, especially egg yolk and orange juice. I am overwhelmed with guilt and dash in to find the baby (sometimes in a crib, sometimes in a carriage down in a dark, dank, stray-cat ridden basement.) I am relieved and amazed to see the baby smiling up at me, plump and contented.

I used my old self therapy techniques a few times and uncovered guilt at being an inadequate mother to my own children.

A. The first time I tried gestalt therapy on it was in my first workshop with Fritz Perls.

Muriel: Are you alright? I was so worried about you. I'm sorry I forgot you.

Baby: (Smiling, relaxed) I feel fine. Don't worry about me. I'm happy.
(Fritz asks if the baby can get up and walk)

Baby: I don't want to. I don't even want to sit up. I like it here. Muriel, stop worrying about me.

I was surprised at this, but did not understand the significance of it. After my first gestalt workshop with Fritz, I began to experiment with gestalt self therapy.

B. Next time I had the same dream, I tried to discover what part of me the baby represented.

Muriel: Thank God you seem healthy and happy. I was so worried about you. All you've had is milk, and you've been cooped up in that crib with no fresh air.

Baby: You're depriving me. I need eggs and orange juice.

Muriel: But you look so healthy and contented.

Baby: Yes, I can survive on milk but I can't grow. Not without other foods.

26

(Here I remembered my own psychological test reports: "She is creative, but might be more creative were she not so driven to produce . . . she may to some extent be suppressing an underlying need to turn her attention in part away from people and toward her own inner self, e.g., through some artistic pursuit." I changed the baby to Little Muriel.)

Little M: I have lots of milk: books to read and self esteem from love and success. But you're too busy to feed me real food so I can't grow. I can't be really creative.

Muriel: What do you want, what do you need to grow?

Little M: You know what I need. You've known ever since you took those tests. I need fun and music and dancing and nature.

Muriel: I know, but I don't have time.

Little M: Stop working so hard. Stop *thinking* so much. You're not fair to me. Stop being so compulsive. Take care of me, damn you.

Muriel: I did take care of you. Where would you be without me? When you were in those foster homes I grew up fast and learned to figure people out. I was your parent. Don't blame me now. I can't help it if I learned to think too much.

C. The next time I worked on the dream was in another of Fritz's workshops. This time Fritz told me to talk to the dream.

Muriel: Stop haunting me. Leave me alone.

Baby: You're neglecting me. You don't have time for me.

Muriel: Where would you be without me. I was a father and a mother to you. Oh my God, I sound just like my father (laughing out loud). That's his voice.

27

Father: I was a father and a mother to you. Be grateful.

Muriel: That's a lie. What did you ever do for me? You boarded me out with strangers. I was alone all those terrible years.

Father: But I always visited you weekends.

Muriel: Big deal! You never gave a damn how I was treated, what happened to me during the week. You conveniently closed your eyes. I managed to survive without you.
(I went back to the baby.)

Baby: I managed to survive without you. I don't need you. I'm getting along fine. Don't be such a fool. Stop trying so hard to understand me. I'm healthy and happy.

Fritz: The baby is the healthiest part of you.

Little by little I began to change after that. Some of the changes were deliberate decisions, some came by themselves, I started buying more records, allowing myself time to dance more often. I began to give the baby, the non-thinking part of me, more freedom. In my workshops I became more of a participant on an emotional level, trusting my intuition more, relying less on the computer in my head, and the workshops improved in effectiveness for my students. Evidently Fritz was right: the baby is the healthiest part of me, my feelings are more useful than my intellect in working with people.

III. ENCOUNTERS WITH PEOPLE

Most of the gestalt self therapy I do is based on irrational or painful feelings about people. This gives me a practical tool for interpersonal relations. Just as with my other self therapy techniques [4], each time I work through an apparent feeling toward someone, it evaporates and I am then able to relate to him in a rational way.

Here are five steps, a loose guideline for gestalt self

therapy. You may move back and forth from one step to another, but in general it feels like this:

How to Experience an Inner Conflict

I. Notice an intense and/or painful feeling about a person or event: anger, fear, hurt, disapproval, jealousy, envy, dependence, helplessness, controlling, controlled; or a neurotic symptom aroused by that person: anxiety, depression or obsessive thinking, all three of which are covers for a hidden emotion; or physical symptoms: signs of tension, psychosomatic illness.

II. Have an imaginary confrontation with that person, playing each role alternately. I change seats and bodily stance each time I change roles. Some of my students find this distracting, and do better simply talking in different voices.

Some people feel freer with an audience of self therapy group members, others can only do it alone in complete privacy. I do best with one other person with whom I feel safe; who will not be bored or judgmental.

With a larger audience I am afraid of taking too much time. Alone, I cannot seem to take myself seriously enough to get into it; it feels boring and dead. I always keep my eyes closed to avoid thinking about my audience and to get deeper into my fantasies.

1) Speak aloud the thoughts of both people more frankly than possible in real life.
2) Speak thoughts you imagine the other may be thinking, especially those thoughts which trouble you, even if, *especially* if, the Adult in you says you are being irrational, just projecting. It is the projections we are after.
3) Exaggerate, caricature both sides. I use my whole body to do this, gesticulating, making faces, standing up tall or cringing on the floor.
4) Stay with this encounter until you have felt as

29

deeply as possible. You will reach a peak of emotion and then start cooling off. Just before you cool off, go on to the next step.

III. Ask yourself, "Who did this to whom?" Change one side to a person or persons from a) your present life, b) your past. Follow 1, 2, 3, and 4 in step II above.

IV. Change both people to two sides of yourself. Follow 2, 3, and 4 as above.

V. "What is my inner conflict?" This is where you are now. Remember to go back and experience this impasse whenever you have an opportunity.
And: "What small compromises can I make between these opposing forces at this stage?"

The following is an example of how I used gestalt self therapy to explore an irrational feeling after an encounter with a student.

The background

In one of my workshops, Jill received valuable negative feedback from the group: She continually frustrated them in three ways: she kept talking compulsively in vague generalities which bored them and never told them how she felt about anything that was happening—the only thing they wanted to hear. She never listened when they tried to tell her their own feelings, and she seemed to be trying to stop them from feeling. True to her pattern, Jill used these same tactics to avoid hearing this feedback.

She was a likeable woman and the group cared about her. They were frustrated by her refusal to hear them. But I was more frustrated than anyone else. I had known Jill and her husband for some time and I realized how important this feedback was for her personal life. I had a pretty good idea about the hidden meaning of her pattern, how she got that way, and I was obsessed with the need to make her listen, make her use this experience for growth. I could not stand to see her miss the boat. I had to save her!

So I made time during a break to corner Jill and rapidly

diagnose her position, the meaning of her behavior, the value of group feedback, and a blueprint for self therapy. Jill responded to my words just as she had done to the group's comments. She talked compulsively in an effort to drown me out, dealt only with generalities, refused to recognize her feelings and managed to avoid hearing anything of value. My intensity, added to the group's pressure was evidently more than Jill could bear. She left the workshop a day early. (I later learned that the next week she did self therapy for the first time, so evidently something important was happening.)

When the workshop was over, I began to think obsessively about Jill, rehearsing over and over again in my mind ways of explaining it all to her, persuading, selling my ideas: this is the form my obsessive thinking usually takes.

When the obsessive thinking became a torment, I tried gestalt self therapy. That was Step I, *notice intense or painful feeling* about a person *or a neurotic symptom*: depression, anxiety, obsessive thinking.

Step II. Have an *imaginary confrontation* with that person, playing each role alternately. Speak each person's thoughts aloud. My dialogue with Jill went something like this:

Muriel: Jill, please listen to me. I have such important things to tell you.

Jill: I don't want to hear.

Muriel: Please let me save you. I can't stand to see what you are doing.

Jill: I don't know what you're talking about.

Muriel: Don't you see how you're holding people at arm's length? That's why you're so lonely.

Jill: I don't know what you're all trying to do to me. Leave me alone.

Muriel: We're trying to get near you. We like you. We want to know you better, but you won't let us. Please listen to me. I want to help you. I understand it all and I can explain it all to you.

31

Jill: Leave me alone. Go away. I can't hear you.

Muriel: You need this nourishing food I'm trying to feed you. You're starving.

Jill: I can't swallow your food. Stop forcing it down my throat.

Muriel: Please, please don't push me away. Please don't starve yourself.

Step III. *Who did this to whom?*

Jill: (Shouting) Go away, damn you. You're just like Mrs. L. (the foster mother who force-fed me to the point of vomiting.)
           At this point Jill became Little Muriel and Muriel became Mrs. L.

Mrs. L: (Standing over Little Muriel, screaming, grimacing) EAT IT! EAT IT, damn you. I'll force it down your throat. (Gesture of forcing food down.)

Little M: (Gagging) Please don't. I can't. I would if I could but I can't.

Mrs. L: (Screaming) Eat it, eat it. I'll make you swallow it. I'll beat you if you vomit.

Little M: (On her knees, pleading) Please don't make me. I can't, I can't. Please, please leave me alone.

Step IV. *Change both people to sides of yourself.*

Muriel 1: Stop forcing people. Let them live. Who the hell do you think you are? Damn you.

Muriel 2: But they're so deprived and I know what they need. I have to save them. I have to help them, poor things.

Muriel 1: You lousy hypocrite! Pretending to be so saintly. You're just power mad, that's all.

Muriel 2: No, it's not true. I have to feed those starving people. I can't stand to see them so deprived when I know what they need.

Muriel 1: Goddamned liar. Rotten phony. I hate you (pounding chair). I'll kill you if you don't stop. Stop it. Stop forcing people. Let them live.

Muriel 2: I want to stop, I'm so tired, but I can't.

Step V. What is my inner conflict? The struggle between the drive to save people and the wish to give them the freedom to be autonomous, to move at their own pace.

After this experience I was able to be more relaxed with another student whose resistance had been tormenting me for a long time. I could accept on an emotional level what I had known intellectually for a long time: that only she herself could struggle with her resistance, that it was not my battle.

Appendix II contains ten more examples of gestalt self therapy. All gestalt self therapy dialogues in this chapter and in Appendix II are condensed for teaching purposes. The actual experience takes much longer than is apparent from these examples; all are accompanied by signs of intense emotion.

4. THE SEARCH FOR IDENTITY

MOST OF US are afraid to face our inner conflicts. We prefer to oversimplify, to know only one side of ourselves, blinding ourselves to the other side and seeing ourselves as two-dimensional. When you fail to see yourself in the round, you are unaware of your true identity. As a result of this blindness you cannot achieve genuine intimacy with anyone. How can you be honest with others when you lie to yourself? And you clutter up your life with neurotic defenses (symptoms) to cover up your hidden side. The more neurotic you are, the more areas of your life are contaminated by these hidden conflicts and the more desperately you avoid experiencing them.

To be an authentic person is to know who you really are, to experience the conflicting sides of your personality. Self therapy (and especially gestalt self therapy) is a path to self knowledge.

When you reach a hidden facet of yourself and realize how you have been lying to yourself and others all these years, you may begin to feel ashamed. This is the time to remember that you did not invent this system of defenses out of thin air, just for fun. You developed this system in childhood in order to survive. Each of us received, long ago, a subtle, probably nonverbal message from people on whom we were dependent. Perhaps unconsciously, they imposed this distortion on our personalities with threats of rejection or abandonment. We were so helpless and dependent that we had no other choice. Therefore, each time you let yourself go into hidden feelings in self therapy be sure to come back to your Adult self again. The Adult can remind you that your distortions once served a vital purpose—survival. If, after each self therapy experience, you forget to come back to the Adult, the cruel Parent will take control and punish you with self-hatred, shame, or guilt about those defenses. If your Adult is too weak, use your therapist, or some other adult

34

you respect, as a model. Try to remember his rational words at this time.

That system of screening out whole parts of yourself which once was essential has now outlived its usefulness and cripples you today. If you dare to experience the forbidden sides of your inner conflicts, you can stop limping around on one leg. You can throw away those crutches (defenses) and run and skip and dance like a whole person.

A whole person is three-dimensional, a complex bundle of many traits. The neurotic, in his damaged areas, is artificial, two-dimensional, because in screening out one side of an inner conflict he exaggerates the other. He is a caricature of a whole person.

When you smother one part of yourself it struggles for release and pushes you into self-defeating behavior. One self-defeating pattern is your tendency to gravitate toward someone who seems to be living out your forbidden trait (someone who has defenses opposite to yours) and you over-react to that trait. You may idealize and over-evaluate that trait and become infatuated with him or you may despise it and feel compelled to change him. Often you do both: nag him to change while setting him up to act out the very behavior you are complaining about [4].

Here are a few examples of conflicts people avoid by living out only one side and screening out the other:

Gentle versus *Tough*.

The neurotically *gentle* person is passive at inappropriate times and suffers physical symptoms (headaches, etc.) when he swallows his responses to painful situations. Under his gentleness is an accumulation of rage. Each act of appeasement, which he experiences as degrading, adds to that rage. His fantasy is that he is a dangerous person and that if he ever dared feel that rage it would overpower him and force him to act it out in some terrible way. This is a self-fulfilling prophesy, since the long periods of self discipline inevitably lead to occasional violent outbursts. The compulsively gentle person grew up in a home where expression of anger was too dangerous, and he over-learned his lesson.

35

The compulsively *tough* person uses pseudo-toughness to cover gentleness of which he is ashamed. As a child, he rushed into adolescent rebellion too early, long before he was developmentally ready for independence. He was cynical and angry with his parents at an age when children need to develop trust. Today he is afraid to let himself feel the longing for love and protection which he smothered long ago in order to avoid disappointment. He over-reacts to gentle people, labeling them weak, and despising their appeasing ways. His hidden fear is that he may give in and act like them, lose the toughness and strength which kept him going in childhood. Like all neurotics, he is still fighting a battle which belongs to the past.

The *gentle* person is often impressed by the tough one, enjoying a vicarious satisfaction in the "strong" acting-out behavior because of his own hidden anger. The tough one thinks the gentle person is a coward. He does not suspect that this passiveness often covers more fear of his own anger than of others.

Trusting versus *Suspicious*.

The neurotically *trusting* person hides his head in the sand like an ostrich, for fear of facing reality. He wants to believe that "all is for the best in this best of all possible worlds" and his willful blindness makes him a victim of painful surprises. A simple, naive parent acted as a model for him and also deliberately taught him to ignore painful family realities.

The *suspicious* person tries to avoid surprises. He sees the world as hostile and threatening, full of people who want to exploit him, and he is always on the alert to protect himself. In a frantic effort to avoid pain, he outsmarts himself. He distorts reality to fit his preconceived ideas and creates the very situation he dreads. By rejecting others, he pushes them away and then experiences them as rejecting; by interpreting their warmth as coldness he frustrates them so they lose that warmth; by blaming and accusing unjustly he puts them on the defensive against him. The suspicious person is blind to most of the good things available and goes through life collecting grievances. Deceitful, subtly depriving parents taught him this cynicism early in life and now he cannot believe that the whole world is not exactly like his original family.

Clever versus *Stupid.*

The compulsively *clever* person once was a child of one stupid parent whom he could easily outwit and another parent who valued him for his cleverness alone. Today he is out of touch with his feelings and has little respect or interest in the emotional life. He attempts (and fails!) to solve interpersonal relations on a purely intellectual level. He overevaluates his own intelligence, is not as clever as he thinks he is and tries compulsively to impress himself and others with his intellect.

The compulsively *stupid* person has a neurotic need to appear stupid to himself and others, despite a basically good mind. In early childhood he received the subtle message from a parent that he could be loved only in the role of fool. Playing stupid serves several purposes: a) it has survival value b) by exaggerating his stupidity he can frustrate and punish the parent who imposed it. He becomes a caricature of the parent's demand, as if to say, "O.K., if this is what you want, you'll get it. I'll rub your nose in it." Today he still follows that old pattern and tends to be impressed by one who is compulsively *clever* (see above), and to marry him, since the clever one is perfectly suited to play the parent's role. The *clever* one needs someone to whom he can feel superior; the *stupid* one needs someone to frustrate with apparent foolishness. Each accepts the other at his own evaluation.

If the *stupid* person outgrows his neurotic tendency and begins to know himself, he will begin to see reality clearly. He will no longer be impressed by the other's cleverness. Unless his partner can grow too, the marriage will deteriorate.

Beautiful versus *Ugly.*

This inner conflict occurs in men and women, but more frequently in women because our culture equates female market value with physical beauty. The compulsively *ugly* woman received a message early in life, often from a beautiful mother afraid of competition, that she would be accepted only in the role of Plain Jane. The child continues to play that role all her life, compulsively slovenly, dowdy, and usually obese. With a little effort she could be attractive, but she obeys that hidden command of long ago. This pattern, like that of the *stupid* one described earlier, serves two purposes: a) it once had survival value and b) it frustrates and embarrasses her mother whose desperate efforts to teach her good grooming, etc. fall on deaf ears as if to say, "You wanted an ugly daughter? O.K., you shall have one."

The obsessively *beautiful* woman was once a little girl whose mother, unable to love her as an individual, delighted in dressing her up and exhibiting her as if she were a doll. Today this woman believes that only her beauty has any value, that she has nothing else to offer. Her fanatical obsession with her appearance, and her belief that no one could be interested in anything else about her, colors her attitude with men so that she can never achieve true intimacy with them. Her aura of the professional beauty tends to scare off a man who wants a real relationship and attracts one who needs a conspicuously beautiful woman in order to bolster up his self esteem. Now she is back again with someone like her mother who can value her for her looks alone. This woman lives in dread of old age and the loss of beauty which to her spells loss of love and identity.

Independent versus *Dependent*.

I myself am an example of the neurotically *independent* person. Lately I am becoming more and more aware that my drive for independence is irrational and all-pervasive. It is painful for me to accept help and, until very recently, has been almost impossible to ask for it.

The compulsively *dependent* person, the "clinging vine," is living out his fantasy of the helpless child, as if all sources of strength and pleasure come from others. Sometimes this is a person whose mother was one of those women who can only love babies and lose interest in their children as soon as they begin to develop self-reliance. Without a father who can love him as he grows more self-reliant, this child chooses to live out the role of chronic baby. This pattern is easily developed in a girl, since the culture accepts helplessness in women more comfortably than in men.

She tends to gravitate to people who enjoy feeling protective and superior and her marriage usually resembles a Parent-Child relationship. Each feeds into the other's pattern while complaining bitterly about one another. ("He's so bossy, he won't give me any freedom." and "She's so childish, I can't trust her to make any important decisions.")

Sensitive versus *Good Sport*

I have noticed that the person who prides himself on being a *sensitive* plant is usually rather insensitive to other people's feelings. He acts as if he is the only vulnerable person around. He is a grievance collector, always on the alert for the careless word or deed to which he instantly responds with resentment, labeled "hurt." His over-reaction to others is a weapon to control them with punishment ("You cruel monster!") or blackmail, ("Now I feel like killing myself!").

The "sensitive" person usually marries the *good sport* who is impressed by the dramatic show of feeling at first, but gradually becomes hardened and unresponsive. This callousness stimulates the "sensitive" one to greater efforts, more hysterical proof of suffering, which forces the other to further withdrawal, etc.

I am an example of the *good sport*. This year I have become aware of my lifelong struggle to avoid feeling any kind of helplessness or humiliation. Whenever someone does anything that might hurt me, I turn off my feelings and become a cold computer, a thinking machine, completely unaware that I am hurt. The other person then feels inadequate, as if he is beneath me and has no power to move me. He is driven to try harder to reach me. Eventually my coldness turns into indignant, self-righteous anger, like a scolding Parent; a perfect disguise for the hurt, degraded Child underneath.

When I am faced with an impossible task, I avoid feeling helpless by becoming a computer which won't stop, tortured by obsessive thinking which can only be relieved by self therapy.

Oversexed versus *Undersexed.*

The apparently *oversexed* person was once a child who felt rejected by his parent of the same sex. On a hidden level, he craves that parent's love all his life and, like most adult neurotics, tends to sexualize that love. Hidden beneath his apparent hypersexuality and promiscuity is a Child vainly seeking a parent's love. He searches for it in people of the *opposite* sex because:

a) he has learned to fear and distrust the parent of his own sex,
b) his parent of the opposite sex seemed to offer a promise of intimacy, warmth, and protection (which was never fulfilled),
c) he is ashamed of that longing for love from his rejecting parent and keeps it hidden with layers of apparent hatred.

The *oversexed* person is irrational in friendships with people of the same sex. The hidden craving for love and fear of the original parent of the same sex may be covered with all or any of the following apparent emotions: blanket distrust and intense discomfort with all people of the same sex; projecting his own sexualized craving for love on the other person, fantasizing that the other has homosexual designs on him.

The neurotically *undersexed* person views his parent of the same sex as bad and sexually seductive. He tries desperately to be different from that parent by acting as nonsexual as possible. The Child within him, however, still longs for love from that parent and he seeks it in friendships. These relationships tend to frustrate him because of his transference on his friend and the resulting distortion. He idealizes his friend, puts him on a pedestal, suffers continual hurt, resentment and jealousy from imagined slights. This puts too great a burden of guilt and helplessness on his friend and prevents a peer relationship.

Authoritarian versus *"Democratic."*

The *authoritarian* person hides feelings of inadequacy under a cloak of apparent smugness. He is most domineering and bossy when threatened with feelings of indecision and helplessness. In childhood he was at the mercy of a degrading parent who undermined his faith in himself. Today he imitates that parent, blustering and bullying, in an attempt to disguise his inner lack of courage and conviction.

The neurotically *"democratic"* person too, has few convictions and little courage. He has difficulty making decisions and is rarely certain about the rightness of any path. He tends to "pass the buck," put responsibility on others. In parenthood, he avoids responsibility even when his children's welfare may be at stake. He wants to believe that he and his children are all equal, all kids together, and in his avoidance of leadership, may deprive them of basic emotional security. The "democratic" person *consciously* experiences his fantasies of helplessness. He often forms a close relationship with the authoritarian person whose own fantasies of helplessness are *unconscious*. The "democratic" one reneges on responsibility and leaves a vacuum which the authoritarian one fills. Each complains about the other's trait ("He's so bossy!" "She's so weak!") while acting in ways to encourage that behavior in one another.

To sum up: in certain damaged areas of your personality you have developed exaggerated traits hiding their opposite. You tend to be irrational in these damaged areas: problem-solving and interpersonal relationships are contaminated by the inner conflict between the two extremes—the side you compulsively act out versus the forbidden, hidden side. At such times, you cannot use your intelligence and experience: you will act in self-defeating ways and then feel frustrated, ashamed, guilty or helpless.

41

GESTALT SELF THERAPY
HOW TO FIND YOUR TRUE IDENTITY

I. Self therapy (described in appendix I) on self-defeating behavior.

II. Look forward to similar experiences.

III. *Gestalt* self therapy on inner conflict.

IV. Make some small change in behavior.

I. When you feel guilt, shame, frustration, or helplessness after some self-defeating behavior, *use that apparent emotion for self therapy.* Each time you explore a painful emotion and feel what is hidden beneath it, you become more self-aware.

II. *Look forward to similar experiences,* similar failures to solve problems in this area, and use them for further self therapy. Use your new self-knowledge to discover your exaggerated personality trait.

III. *In gestalt self therapy, have a dialogue between two sides of yourself.* Now that you are aware of your exaggerated trait, you can assume that there is an opposite, hidden side. Play through the conflict between the side you have been living out and the forbidden side: stupid versus clever, beautiful versus ugly, sexy versus sexless, etc. Listen to the sound of your voice when you play the forbidden side. Whom from your past does that voice remind you of? Play that person. Who, in childhood, gave you a message forbidding you to live that hidden side? Have a dialogue with him; be the child you once were.

IV. *You can make some small change in your real life behavior* after each gestalt self therapy experience, after each time you get a real glimpse of your hidden side.

Remember that insight alone will not change you. It is up to you to assume some conscious responsibility. Watch for opportunities to *experiment with new behavior.* Next time you are tempted to act out that exaggerated trait, of which you are now aware, try a slight modification of your usual behavior and see how it feels. Do *not* set up an entirely new program for yourself; that is likely to be mere acting out of your hidden side (see "The Inner Conflict"). Just try something new on for size and then notice how the new behavior makes you feel. Remember you may have to do gestalt self therapy many, many times on the same trait, but each time you will discover more freedom to experiment in new behavior; you will begin to lose that old rigidity which is characteristic of neurotic behavior. Eventually, with hard work in self therapy and practice in new ways, you will stop being a two-dimensional caricature and become a whole person. Meanwhile, during this slow period of learning and practicing you will gradually find yourself shedding all kinds of neurotic symptoms, peeling away layers of unnecessary defenses accumulated through the years.

Example: Earlier in this chapter I mentioned my neurotic need to be independent and my compulsive good sportsmanship. I had always considered these to be virtues, proud that I was not easily hurt, proud of my self reliance. I never thought to examine these traits, to consider them irrational, until workshop members began to complain. Every once in a while some student would accuse me of coldness. At first I thought he must be distorting, but when each time, the group agreed, I had to pay attention to what was happening. I was shocked to think I had unwittingly hurt my own students with coldness. Many of them had transferences on me and so were especially vulnerable to rejection. Besides, this was a horrid contradiction of my self image—the warm, loving Jewish Mother figure.

I. Each time I heard that accusation, I went back to the exact moment they described, and worked on it in self therapy. What happened just before that? What was I trying not to feel? And each time I discovered I had been hiding either hurt or helplessness, covering up with the pseudo-strength of cool intellectualizing. Whenever I was hurt or helpless I instantly slipped into my "helping" role: thinking, analyzing, teaching and invulnerable—acting like a computer to avoid feeling weakness. I did not realize how cold I appeared.

After several such encounters, where my students' complaints pushed me into self therapy, I became aware that this avoidance of hurt and helplessness was self defeating. There I was, trying to provide a warm, supportive atmosphere where people could feel safe enough to do self therapy, and instead I was frightening them with my coldness. I was trying to teach them to be authentic while lying to myself, pretending to be a superwoman, never hurt, never weak. Now I began to pay attention, to become more and more aware of the ways I avoided feeling hurt. After a while I saw how this pattern involved my problem with anger.

Long ago I had discovered (in self therapy) an irrational fear of my own anger, the unconscious fantasy that I am a dangerous person. It is still difficult for me to know when I am angry, although I am improving, but I still avoid showing anger even when I can feel it. When anger becomes obsessive, when I cannot get it out of my mind, I use it for gestalt self therapy. Each time I explore obsessive anger, I discover feelings of weakness—hurt, helplessness, sometimes fear—underneath. Obsessive anger is always pseudo-anger for me.

For most people who avoid acting out anger in general, our children are our natural victims. I didn't do much spanking (fear of my dangerous powers stopped me very soon) but I certainly did a lot of yelling and scared my poor kids.

I rarely act out *genuine* anger. Whenever I am swept up into impulsive behavior by "anger" it is fake, pseudo-anger, a cover for weakness—for hurt, helplessness or fear. I know now (too late!) that I frightened my little girls when I was hiding feelings of inadequacy, helplessness, or hurt.

II. Now that I see my pattern of avoiding hidden weakness with coldness and pseudo-anger, I *am on the alert for more opportunities to explore it.* Whenever I notice myself feeling cold toward someone I care about, and whenever I am obsessed with anger, I have an imaginary encounter with that person in gestalt self therapy, and follow my usual path (see chapter, "Gestalt Self Therapy.") Little by little I am uncovering bits and pieces of my hidden self. Each time I go back to my childhood I see how essential that pseudo-strength once was for me.

44

THE SEARCH FOR IDENTITY

For years in self therapy I have cried in sympathy for my five-year-old self, deserted by Mother, placed in strange foster homes, at the mercy of rejecting and sometimes cruel grown-ups, just as I cry for other helpless children. Until now I had never let myself go back and actually *experience the helplessness* of that position. I knew I had to do that, feel the opposite side of my apparent strength and independence. The first few times I began to follow that downward path I trembled with anxiety: so terrifying to let myself feel weak; I might get stuck there and never escape to my safe adult life again. But I have been going back again and again, whenever the opportunity arrives, whenever I need to explore my pseudo-strength.

I know now that in those early years I never dared feel my real helplessness. A small child hasn't the strength to let himself experience certain kinds of pain. He finds ways to avoid it. Those were the days when I developed the pattern of acting like a computer to avoid feeling helpless. Like an anthropologist living among savage tribes, in each new foster home I studied my new parents and learned how to handle them. I learned to hide my thoughts and feelings, to appear to be whatever kind of little girl they wanted. I learned to make new friends each time I changed homes and to keep my peculiar home life secret from them. I learned how to get warmth and approval from teachers and other children's mothers. And all the time I concentrated on my strength, ignored my weakness.

III. In gestalt self therapy I went back to my five-year-old self, vainly pleading with Mother to come back; to my seven-year-old self begging my foster mother to stop beating me; and finally to my stubborn adolescent self, biting my lip to avoid crying, presenting a cold mask during my stepmother's degrading tirades, frustrating her attempts to break me down. I could see now how I was stuck in that adolescent role of cold indifference to anyone who tried to hurt me. To show hurt or helplessness, even to feel it, meant going back to early childhood, begging for mercy that never came. Until I stumbled on it in self therapy, I forgot that I had ever been foolish and weak enough to abase myself that way. I had buried those failures deep inside where they channeled themselves through my neurotic symptoms.

I could see now the purpose of those old defenses, the coldness, the pseudo-anger. My main task in those days was to maintain my self esteem, to avoid feeling degraded and helpless. It was a good system and it worked for me. It helped me move from childhood to adolescence. Now my Adult mind saw how foolish it was to keep struggling for something I already had, what an anachronism it was to wear those worn-out, out-grown clothes just because I once needed them. No one in my present life can degrade me, can change my self image. They can only *hurt* me. I can afford to feel hurt now; I am strong enough; I am an Adult and I need to prove that to the frightened Child within me.

IV. I set an assignment for myself—to let myself feel hurt or helpless when necessary. This is a report of Work in Progress. It is still an effort of will for me to notice myself thinking too fast, like a computer; to pay attention to a certain "crawly" feeling, like a cold chill, in my scalp; to say "Something's bothering me; maybe I'm hurt," and then to feel my face breaking up, to let go of the cool, superior mask, to feel and show the hurt.

I am learning to recognize symptoms of disguised helplessness too. The apparent feeling is frustration, sometimes anger. Suddenly I cannot tolerate the other person's behavior and I have an overwhelming desire to control him, to teach him, to *make* him do it right! I usually feel shaky inside and sometimes I tremble visibly. (In the days when I avoided feeling the helplessness and just felt frustrated and angry, that trembling, ironically enough, looked to observers like a different kind of weakness—fear.)

I am learning to let go, to feel the helplessness; and then the frustration, the anger and need to control all disappear. Then I can be a rational person; I can live and let live, instead of controlling.

From time to time I try to let people help me when they want to. Sometimes I experience mild anxiety symptoms and used them for self therapy, feel the craving for self reliance, the old fear of dependency.

46

THE SEARCH FOR IDENTITY

Learning to live out the hidden side of myself, the "weak" side, is a task far from completed. I know I have a long way to go. Whenever I dare to feel hurt or helpless, whenever I allow someone to help me perform a task I could do myself, it is by voluntary effort. I still tend to act out the "strong" side most of the time and then I depend on the discipline of gestalt self therapy to explore my apparent feelings—the cold, obsessive thinking or the anger—and go back to the hidden weakness. After each of these therapeutic experiences I am free for the time being of the obsession, and I can apologize to anyone I might have hurt while I was caught up in the apparent emotion.

How long will it take for me to outgrow my childish need to maintain my self respect by living a two-dimensional life in the area of strength versus weakness? Will I ever outgrow it, or must I practice constant vigilance all my life to avoid acting out in self-defeating ways? I do not know, but I have faith in the system; I *did* outgrow my shame pattern (see "The Courage to Fail"). Maybe this too will pass.

Meanwhile, I have no other choice but to continue the work of self therapy and experimentation with new behavior based on increased self awareness. Although I am damaged in this area, my goal is to act like a rational being despite my neurotic tendencies; to solve problems with my Adult mind rather than to be led by the idiot Child within me; to live in the present, not in the past.

I see certain changes even now. I can feel hurt and helplessness spontaneously much more frequently, even though it is not always convenient to show it. I can ask for help occasionally from people who love me. I suffer less from obsessive thinking now that I depend less on it as a defense. Certain other symptoms are letting up too, symptoms I never before connected with this pattern. I used to get headaches when my drive to "save" someone conflicted with a hidden feeling of helplessness. Now, when I feel the constriction in my head, I can let myself recognize my helplessness, my inability to accomplish the impossible, and I no longer "need" the headache.

Another bonus is my new freedom to read fiction. Reading has always been my greatest source of release and refreshment, and all my life I read fiction avidly. But in recent years I had been narrowing myself down to books which cannot move me. My work with real people and their personal tragedies seemed all I could take. I dreaded emotional involvement with characters in fiction. I began to limit myself to those few novels whose authors promised not to wring my heartstrings. I turned to nonfiction, especially history. But even there I kept stumbling on vivid accounts of suffering people from the past and these pushed me into headache or depression.

In the last few months I have gone back to my early reading pattern. I can enjoy many more books of fiction and no longer require hours in the library to choose enough "safe" books to last me. Evidently my new ability to experience helplessness is widening this avenue of recreation. Until recently novels stirred up too much hidden helplessness.

Horses wear "blinders" to protect them from frightening objects, to keep their vision straight ahead on the road. The neurotic wears blinders to avoid seeing anything that might arouse a hidden feeling. The more hidden feelings you have, the more things you avoid seeing, and the fewer experiences you allow yourself. Life becomes a long, boring road where you can only put one foot in front of the other, missing all the fun and excitement. I am aware of some of the areas where I still wear blinders and I hope to free myself further. Meanwhile, I am grateful to be free of my restriction on reading. We punish ourselves the same ways the parents in our lives once punished us. My foster mother tore up my library card and deprived me of books at a time when I needed that escape from my daily life. I have been depriving myself of books, my most valuable source of relaxation.

Earlier in this chapter I stated that we tend to gravitate to people who live out our own forbidden characteristics. Years ago Fritz Perls told me, "You will not be a good therapist until you stop being so damned helpful." I know now that I have been drawn to the apparent helplessness in some people and have encouraged their dependence on me by being too "helpful." Nowadays I am more aware of their hidden strength. I am learning to let go, to allow my students to stay in the therapeutic impasse without rushing in to "rescue" them; to let them struggle with their conflicts and find their own way out. I am beginning to act more like a teacher of self therapy and less like the stereotype of the Jewish Mother. Now that I can face my own hidden weakness I am aware of others' hidden strength even when that strength is disguised as weakness.

This change in behavior based on inner growth is painful for some students. When "identified patients" in family therapy [7] [8] begin to change, others in the family become uncomfortable. The status quo is upset. When one member of a marriage gets healthy enough to stop playing neurotic games the other suffers. Unless he too can grow and change, the relationship deteriorates [5].

5. SELF DISCIPLINE

TO MOST of us self discipline is a puritanical concept: "I hate to do this and *therefore* I should force myself. If I make myself do the thing I hate or fear it will be good for me; it will strengthen my character." That word "should" is a danger signal. Whenever you find yourself blindly obeying, against enormous resistance, the "shoulds" in your head, it is time to sort out the hidden voices before rushing into impulsive action.

Try gestalt self therapy. Have a dialogue between the Parent and the Child within you and find out what is going on. Be the Parent, scolding, nagging, judging: "You *should* do this because it is the proper thing to do. What's the matter with you? Hurry up! Stop dragging your feet. Shame on you for being so bad (or stupid or crazy)!" Stay in the Parent role long enough to whip up some feeling. Then be the Child. You will find the Child functioning in one of three ways:

1. Frightened, pleading for mercy: "I'm doing the best I can. Please stop punishing me. You're demanding too much of me. I can't live up to your standards. I'm sorry."

2. Appeasing, manipulating, trying to avoid punishment: "Yes, you are so right and I am so wrong. I *am* bad (or stupid or crazy); that's why I can't do it." Here the Child is manipulating the Parent, pretending to agree in order to shut the Parent up.

3. Rebellious Adolescent: "To Hell with you! I won't do it your way. I want to have fun. I'm not afraid of you."

Stay in this Parent-Child struggle as long as it generates feelings. Next, try to hear whose actual voice from the past the Parent reminds you of. Who, in your past or present life, makes such demands on you, punishes you this way? Mother? Father? Teacher? Sibling? Friend? Have an encounter with that other person, playing both him and your-self.

Next stage: play both sides of yourself. One side is like that other person in your life. (Further on in this chapter I will explain how to compromise between these extremes.)

Suppose you refuse to experience the inner struggle, by-pass self therapy and simply bull your way through; "dis-cipline" yourself to do the thing you hate or fear, without any self awareness. These are the times you use self discipline in one or more self-defeating ways: I. Apparent obedience to the Parent, or II. disobedience.

I. Apparent obedience. In this case, the hidden Child, whose voice you are refusing to hear, makes itself known in one or both of two ways:

1. Neurotic symptoms:
    a. Emotional: anxiety, depression, irritability, ob-sessive thinking, inappropriate emotion.
    b. Physical: headache, physical tension, psycho-matic illness.

2. Sabotaging the Parent with: difficulty in concentra-tion, forgetfulness, tardiness, stupidity, boredom, physical disability (see 1.b. above). Any of these symptoms stops the action. Read THE ADJUSTED AMERICAN [11] for further discussion of unconscious sabotage.

II. Disobeying the Parent. Here, too, there are two ways to react.

1. Appeasing and manipulating the Parent to avoid punishment: "Oh, well, I'm so bad (stupid or crazy) that I simply can't discipline myself. I'm just a failure. What can I do? I can't help myself."

The Existentialists believe we are what we are becoming. Although you are largely a product of past experiences, you do have a small, precious area of free will. You can make choices. Each day presents an opportunity to make some small decision which will either help you to grow or set you back.

The Talmud interprets the biblical statement, "God made

man in His own image," to mean, He gave man the intelligence to know right from wrong and the strength to make choices. Each time a man chooses the right way it becomes easier for him to make the right choice next time. But each wrong step makes it more difficult to get on the right path in the future.

True, we are victims of past experiences which helped form our characters, but we are not finished products; we are not *entirely* made by the past. Present and future experiences continue to make us what we are becoming and we have a small, precious measure of control over these new experiences. We can choose experiences to help us grow.

Each time I do something to reinforce the punishing Parent voice in my head, each time I prove to myself how bad, stupid or crazy I am, I am taking a backward step; the struggle for growth becomes harder. Some people think they can separate themselves from their actions: "I may be forced to do bad things, but I will not let them touch me. I will rise above them. I will keep my soul pure even though my actions are degrading." This is a dangerous fantasy and can lead to mental illness. Bruno Bettelheim [21] explains that people *are* what they *do*.

Each time I make a decision and perform an action appropriate for the kind of person I want to be, I make it a little easier to become that person. Understand that here I am discussing *actions, behavior*—not *feelings and thoughts*. If I try to limit my ideas and emotions to those appropriate to the person I hope to be, I am merely lying to myself, being phony. If I avoid my "bad" thoughts and feelings I not only slow up my progress but I add new neurotic symptoms to my collection. Each inappropriate feeling I let myself experience and explore in self therapy gives me more control over my behavior.

2. Another way to disobey the Parent voice is by acting out the Rebellious Adolescent. The apparent thought is, "I'm tired of conforming to society's demands. I'm free and brave and no matter what anyone says, I'm O.K." The hidden words which come out in self therapy are addressed to the Parent, "To hell with you! I'm tired of trying to

satisfy you. I will not be controlled by you anymore. I'm a big boy now."

Without insight into the hidden battle, you behave as if you were still living in the past, as if your struggle is actually with another person. It seems to you that you can strengthen yourself by fighting off some outside control, the way an adolescent breaks free of his parents. Since this battle belongs to the past, the fact that you are acting it out now shows that it is unfinished business for you. Try to experience it as such, in gestalt self therapy. Begin with the person whom you think is controlling you today. Then change him into someone from your past. Finally, hear the two sides of yourself, the rebel and the undigested lump of Parent: consciously fight that inner battle. You can never undo the past by simply acting out self-defeating behavior in real life situations, only with self therapy and new behavior based on insight.

Whenever you act out in this way, rebel against the Parent in your head without experiencing the inner conflict, you lie to yourself, pretending to be independent of that scolding voice. Whenever you hide one side of yourself, refuse to listen to a voice in your head, you act in self defeating ways. Whenever you blindly act out the Rebellious Adolescent:

a) You are incapable of Adult behavior. You distort reality, you assert yourself in some dramatic way. Then, after this kind of action, if you are self aware, you will begin to feel shame, guilt, or fear. Or you may feel anxiety or depression as a cover for some such painful emotion. This means your behavior has stirred up the punishing Parent in your head to further cruelty.

b) Or you may succeed in projecting your own inner scolding Parent on to someone else. You think others want to force you to feel shame, guilt or fear because of your behavior (and some of them may); you focus on them instead of your own inner struggle. This can become a self-fulfilling prophesy. If you persist in acting out often enough, projecting the inner battle on to the outside world, others will begin to react to you in just those ways: feeling judgmental, disapproving, parental, or simply want to get away from you, depending on their own personal histories and stage of emotional growth.

I have summed up the self-defeating ways we misuse self discipline. What part does self discipline play in the life of the healthy man? No part at all, if we use Maslow's definition of health which is a far cry from mere adjusted normalcy. Maslow says [9] the healthy man, one in a hundred, (further research led him to change that to one in a thousand) feels no contradiction between his intelligence and emotions. Like healthy children who choose healthful foods because they taste good, he intuitively acts in ways that are good for him because they "taste good." The healthy man does not need self discipline in his daily life, does not experience the chronic inner struggle between "want" and "should."

The rest of us neurotics and so-called "normal" people (those with mildly neurotic tendencies), whose emotions are contaminated by old, unfinished experiences, cannot afford to be guided by the Idiot Child within. We depend on self discipline to help us avoid shame, guilt, fear, helplessness; to maintain self respect; to keep growing; hopefully to become less and less dependent on self discipline as we approach real health. One of the main goals of self discipline should be to outgrow it just as a child who depends on parental guidance eventually outgrows the need for such guidance.

The child, in relation to his parents, goes through certain stages in the development of his ethical growth. If he gets stuck along the way and fails to move on, he becomes a neurotic.

STAGE I

The Child

Little Johnny learns to obey his parents because he needs to *keep their love and approval*. Contrary to popular opinion, Johnny does not learn best from punishment [4]. The child ruled by fear alone, without the incentive of maintaining love and approval, tends to become a criminal psychopath [10].

At this stage little Johnny has not yet developed a

conscience. He follows the rules because disobedience threatens loss of love and approval. His guideline for behavior is, "What will Mommy say?" and he expects her to know what he is doing most of the time, even when she is not around. He attributes to her a godlike all-seeing eye.

The Neurotic

Albert is a grown-up functioning on this level. He does what he thinks he "should" do in order to avoid disapproval and loss of love from those who are important to him: his wife, his friends, his therapist. The more irrational he is, the more he tends to see in every Tom, Dick and Harry an important source of approval. Whenever Albert chooses a course of action, he has to consider various people's values.

Of course, like all neurotics, he tends to project on some of them what he once thought were his parents' standards, and on others the feelings of the Child within him. "What would they say if they knew? How will I look to them? Tom may think I'm foolish, laugh at me. If I disobey the rules Dick will think I'm brave. He'll admire me. But Harry will disapprove, think I'm bad. If I follow the rules Dick will sneer at me for being cowardly."

Albert controls his behavior, uses self discipline, in order to control other people's feelings about him.

STAGE II

The Child

In the child's next stage of moral development, he has swallowed whole his parents' values, according to the policy, "If you can't beat 'em, join 'em." Now, he asks himself, "What would Mommy and Daddy think if they knew?" Even if he knows they won't find out, (he is too sophisticated now to believe they have magic powers) this thought is sufficient to guide him. He not only accepts his parents' standards but he distorts and exaggerates them. When his mother says, "Nice little boys don't do that," meaning, "I don't want you to do that," he interprets it to mean, "When you do that you're BAD!" Little girls playing with their dolls caricature their mothers. They scold and punish more fanatically than their mothers. My own little girl, at this stage, rigidly denied herself the ice cream she craved at a nursery school party despite the teacher's coaxing. She was obeying to the letter my "law" against between-meal sweets. When I later tried to explain that a party was a special occasion she was confused and more frustrated than ever. At this stage, black is black and white, white; there are no greys.

When little Johnny has a choice between "want" and "should" and fails to conform to what he sees as his parents' values, he suffers real discomfort. He feels shame, not guilt; he is too young to experience guilt [4]. In order to share the burden of his shame and get some relief he may confess to his mother ("But don't tell Daddy!") or an older sister or brother ("But don't tell Mommy!").

The Neurotic

Barry is a grown-up functioning on this level. He has swallowed whole someone else's standards of behavior and they remain undigested; they are not an integral part of him. The Child and Parent within Barry are struggling all the time. The Child sometimes conforms, sometimes rebels, sometimes sabotages. Unlike Maslow's healthy man, Barry hardly ever does what is good for him because it "tastes good." What is good for him usually tastes bad: he either gulps it down like medicine or spits it out.

Each time Barry faces the conflict between "want" and "should" he asks himself, "If the important people in my life knew, what would they think?" Important people include parents, dead or alive, teachers, friends. Sometimes the question is a conscious one. When the question is unconscious, hidden, he suffers painful indecision or some other neurotic symptom. If he can uncover the hidden question in self therapy, that symptom disappears.

Like Albert (above) Barry has swallowed more than one person's set of values. This sets the stage for more internal conflict: innumerable voices quarreling within him, telling him what's right and wrong. No matter which voice he satisfies, there will always be another scolding, forcing him to feel shame, inadequacy, helplessness, or simply rage at the chronic inability to experience comfortable self respect.

SELF DISCIPLINE

If Barry becomes aware of the inner conflict he has three alternatives:

a) He can escape discomfort by projecting the inner voices on to other people. He can whip up resentment against their real or imagined disapproval. In this case he regresses to the more primitive level of development described in Stage I. He slows up his emotional growth.

b) Or, like little Johnny (the child above) he can "confess" his shame to some safe listener, a friend or therapist, and get enough reassurance to make him feel better. In this case he neither grows nor regresses. He maintains the status quo.

c) Or he can let himself stay with the shame and feel the discomfort. This is the first step toward emotional growth.

STAGE III

The Child

To reach the third stage of ethical development, little Johnny needs a good model. A good model is someone he respects and trusts and leans on, whose own standards are clear-cut; someone who does *not* solve ethical problems with the thought, "Well, I'm not sure what's right and wrong. What would the neighbors say?"

In addition, in order to grow to this stage, Johnny must chew up his parents' values instead of swallowing them whole (as in Stage II). He must digest some of them and discard others. Some will become an integral part of him, together with values gathered from other sources: teachers, friends, books, the mass media, and his own life experiences.

Now when Johnny transgresses his own values, he feels real guilt. The healthier he is, the more easily he can predict which choices will stir up guilt, the more control he has over his behavior, and the closer he is to his genuine guilt feeling with less need to cover it up with neurotic symptoms.

The Neurotic

Madge is a woman functioning at this level to a large extent. But in addition to well-digested, integrated values of her own, she also suffers from the emotional indigestion due to lumps of unchewed rules, "shoulds" left over from her past history. These are based on illogical, unreasonable concepts, anachronistic standards which have nothing to do with her adult thinking processes. They stir up neurotic guilt. You can atone for real guilt, but there is nothing you can do about neurotic guilt except to feel it, and it is usually so buried in layers of neurotic symptoms and pseudo-emotions that you do not know it is there [4]. We generally disguise neurotic guilt with depression, anxiety, anger or some physical symptom. If you explore that symptom and feel the hidden guilt, the symptom disappears.

If you *avoid* feeling neurotic guilt, you will probably act out some self defeating pattern which conflicts with your real, adult values and will then be forced to feel real guilt. That is, when faced with a choice of "want" and "should," you will function either on the level of weak Child (as in Stage II) or rebellious Adolescent. You will choose the path of "want." This serves two purposes:

a) It justifies the chronic irrational guilt whose source is so mysterious to you; it is somehow more satisfying to suffer when you know you have been "bad" than for unknown reasons.

b) It tempts others to punish you, in the unconscious hope that the punishment will atone for the hidden "sin" and bring relief from the neurotic guilt.

This system usually works for a while. Catastrophes like wars and earthquakes bring emotional relief from neurotic symptoms to many people. They can stop punishing themselves with depression, anxiety, etc. while life punishes them in this dramatic way, and, for the time being, they are relieved of the catastrophic expectation, the dread of dire punishment they have awaited all their lives. Unfortunately, when good times return and the emergency is over the neurotic symptoms, which masked that old dread and served as punishment, return.

I have described at length reasons for exploring hidden feelings before trying to exercise self discipline. How do you know when you are failing to function on an adult level, when the inner conflict will interfere with good resolutions? When is it important to use self therapy?

Ask yourself, "What is the *reason* for my choice?" If you are doing this simply because you fear or hate it, if you are deliberately forcing yourself into it because you think it will be "good" for you, that is a clue that you are blindly obeying the cruel Parent, trying to break the Child's spirit. The Child will probably sabotage your efforts.

This is how sabotage feels. Once, when I was trying to write an article, I set aside an hour each morning for this task, a system that usually works for me. But several days in a row, each time I sat down at the typewriter my teeth began to ache, a sign of tension. Each day I tried to do self therapy, tried to find out what feeling I might be warding off, but I could not experience anything except aching teeth and a greater than usual reluctance to write. Each time I left the typewriter, gave up writing for that day, the symptom disappeared. For some unknown reason, the Child within me sabotaged my efforts to write for an entire week and I *gave in to it*. The following week all was well; I was able to work smoothly and finish my article in record time. (More on my writing problem further on.)

I had no insight into the meaning of the inner conflict. Without self therapy I could not hear what the Child was trying to say. *Pay attention* to the Child within you when it protests in the only way it can even when you don't understand why. Years ago one of my babies cried off and on all day for no apparent reason. She wasn't wet or hungry, no pins were sticking into her; I checked her temperature and it was normal. I had no idea why she was so fretful and so I gave her the only thing that seemed to help—physical comfort. I carried her around most of that day. As long as I held her she seemed to relax and stopped crying. Next day the doctor examined her. He told me she had just been through a day of terrible pain; an abcess burst in her ear.

I try to be as kind to the Child within me as I would be to a baby. When the Child is obviously suffering but cannot speak to me, I do not hesitate to comfort her, give her what she seems to want. I am not afraid to "spoil" her by paying attention to the way she expresses pain—aching teeth, headache, depression, anxiety—any more than I was afraid to spoil my baby when she was obviously suffering.

I try to hear what she is saying by using self therapy when I can. But when I cannot, I simply comfort her. I cut out the self discipline that is evidently tormenting her.

If, when choosing between "should" and "want," you let the Parent run the show you are really making no choice at all. You are simply acting out one side of yourself, ignoring the other. Only the Adult can make genuine choices. The Adult is that part of you that:

a) knows your own personal values, and
b) is aware of reality.

The Adult never says, "Do this because you hate it or are afraid of it. Force yourself. It will strengthen your character." That kind of vague generalization used as an excuse for self discipline always comes from the Parent, the part of you that still functions on an irrational level. The Adult always has a definite, concrete goal in making a choice between "want" and "should." The goal may be an ethical one—an attempt to establish justice, to right a wrong; or it may be an effort to fulfill some vital personal need for intimacy, autonomy, creativity.

The Adult protects you from traumatic surprises. It can predict how much guilt, shame, or inadequacy you may be forced to experience with this particular choice and it has some idea how strong or weak your self-esteem is today, how much guilt, etc. you can tolerate at this time.

Another clue to watch for is terrible indecision with obsessive thinking. When you have too much trouble making a choice between "want" and "should," it means the Adult is asleep. In order to wake it up, take time out to listen to the inner struggle:

Parent: You are bad, (or stupid or crazy) that's why you don't want to do this. That's why you *should* do it. Force yourself. It's good for you to suffer. You deserve it.

Weak Child: I *can't* do it. I'm too bad (or stupid or

crazy). I'll just have to sit here and let you punish me with self hatred.

- Or -

Rebellious   I won't do it. I don't care if I'm bad (or stu-
Adolescent: pid or crazy). I like myself this way and anyone who doesn't like it can lump it.

If you stay with the inner dialogue long enough, the Adult may be able to say, "I'm going to experiment. I'm not absolutely sure I can afford the pain and uncertainty involved in trying out this new behavior, but I'm willing to attempt it. If I can do it I know I will grow and become more like the person I want to be—freer, more fulfilled. Life will be more meaningful."

Sometimes in decision making, the Adult chooses wisely at first and then you hand the reins over to the Parent. When this happens you are setting the stage for either the weak Child or the rebellious Adolescent to sabotage the whole process.

Dieting is a good example. If you are overweight, the Adult has rational reasons for dieting:

1) When you feel more attractive you will be able to have greater intimacy with others;

2) Improved health will make work and play more satisfying;

3) Instead of escaping problems by compulsive eating you will have more opportunities for self awareness and self therapy.

So you go on a diet.

Then the cruel Parent takes over and begins to run the show in one or more of the following ways: chooses a really repulsive diet (you are not allowed the simple animal pleasure of enjoying the little food you do eat); spaces meals so far apart that you feel starved most of the time (a most primitive form of deprivation); omits most healthful foods (you feel physically weak). Naturally, the Child cannot tolerate this kind of deprivation very long. For compulsive eaters, food spells love and survival. Either the weak Child or the rebellious Adolescent will sabotage your good intentions. You find yourself thinking obsessively about meals, craving those forbidden foods, and you go off your diet.

When this happens, if you had not allowed the Parent to control things, the Adult would be alert enough now to say, "Well, O.K. I went off my diet today, but tomorrow is another day. Not much harm done so far. Let's start again." Unfortunately, the Parent has been so cruel and depriving that the Child feels very sorry for itself and becomes so active that the Adult cannot be heard. The Child will say, "O.K. I know I'm weak. I give up." Or the Adolescent, "Oh, to hell with it. Who cares if I'm fat? Dieting isn't worth this misery."

I have dieted most of my life and I always depend on the Adult to choose nutritious foods which give me lots of energy and taste delicious. The Adult helps me wait until I actually feel hunger pangs before sitting down to simple fare; cottage cheese and lettuce can be delicious when you're really hungry. The typical compulsive eater never experiences hunger pangs, because the Adult in him is not functioning. The Child clamors to eat long before he is hungry enough to enjoy an unexciting meal and the Parent serves up the least appetizing menu possible. I know the Child in me can easily feel deprived so I humor her; I shop around for pacifiers. For example, I find that the elaborate process of cracking open sunflower seeds and carefully extracting them one by one is very soothing, and I can consume a great many without gaining weight.

Another way the Adult can help maintain self discipline is to avoid opportunities for recurrent choices and chronic indecision. When my children were small I simplified the mechanics of living, greased the wheels of daily life, with a few uncomplicated rules. For instance, each time I announced that a meal was ready, I repeated the accustomed formula, "and wash your hands." There was no occasion for arguments and decisions. ("But look, my hands are clean. Must I wash them this time?") No struggle with authority, no questions, just a simple, painless ritual based on a decision I, the adult, had made long ago and which the children accepted comfortably.

I handle the Child within me the same way when I discipline myself to write. For me, the hardest part of writing is making the decision to sit right down and do it *now*. I tend to sabotage myself in all kinds of sneaky ways. At the very thought of writing, my household chores suddenly loom large in importance and fascination. Cobwebs, heretofore invisible, beg to be removed; windows and floors crave washing; a chaotic kitchen drawer tempts me to reorganize. I used to struggle anew each day with the problem, "Should I write now or later, or maybe skip this one day?" until I began to treat myself exactly as I did my small children.

Now at a specific hour each morning I stop whatever I am doing and sit down at the typewriter. No need for the daily conflict between "want" and "should." I wrestled a long time with the decision whether or not to write this book, but now that the decision is made, I simply put one foot in front of the other: I write for exactly one hour each morning, no more, no less. Writing for one hour seems a natural creative activity for me. Ideas flow smoothly without stress or strain. But after an hour the work becomes an effort of will, a forced assignment, performed with much physical tension (clenched teeth, etc.), like swimming upstream.

I learned by trial and error that morning is the best time for me to write: words come easily. Later in the day I get bogged down in a compulsive search for the "perfect" word. I torture myself with inhibiting thoughts. Is this idea really important? What about proper sequence of ideas? Am I being logical? Is this hard to understand? . . . and so forth. I know very well that all these problems can be resolved after the first rough draft and that these preoccupations simply interfere with the even flow of ideas, sabotage the work.

I do not *know* why this happens in the afternoon and not in the morning. I have never worked it through in self therapy, but I can make an educated guess about it. Probably at night in dreams I work through enough of my unresolved problems to relieve me of whatever is blocking writing, so that I am free in the morning. By the afternoon I have already become involved in daily problems which stir up hidden conflicts; I become more neurotic, more at the mercy of my unconscious conflicts as the day progresses. Edmund Bergler says this is true for some people with respect to their sexual problems. They are only free to enjoy sex first thing in the morning when they have a taste of health immediately after their dream work.

My Adult self avoids frustrating the Child in me by choosing a time which is most comfortable for writing, just as it chooses the most satisfying menu when I diet. I never forced my children to eat foods they disliked just because they were "good" for them. I experimented until I found which healthful foods they enjoyed.

I do not want to force the Child within me to be uncomfortable. I do not know what she is feeling any more than I knew that my baby had an infected ear, but I do not torment her; I do not tempt her to sabotage my work.

What is self discipline? For one thing, only you yourself know when you are exercising self discipline. To an observer, *compulsive behavior* sometimes appears to be self discipline. For instance, a sloppy housekeeper humbly watching a compulsive one at work may admire what looks to her like self discipline. Only the compulsive housekeeper herself (and her victims, her family) know the truth.

What is the difference between compulsive behavior and self discipline? Freedom. When you act compulsively you feel driven by a mysterious force over which you have little control. There is little satisfaction in the work or the finished product. You are performing an act, not to enrich your life, but merely to ward off anxiety. A compulsive person is like a worshipper in some ancient pagan religion. His religious rites are not a way to celebrate his love for his gods. They are magic spells to protect him against the gods' anger. The compulsive person performs magic rites to ward off punishment from the angry Parent within him.

Self discipline *feels* different. You know you are making a voluntary effort, exercising free will. Your motivation is clear to you; you know what you are trying to accomplish; you have a concrete goal in mind. Compulsive behavior (like ritual in the ancient religion) is blind repetition of an old,

old pattern whose origin you have long forgotten. But self discipline is experiment in new behavior, an attempt to set your foot on a new path.

Sometimes, self discipline may not be apparent to a casual observer. When I was first married, I felt compelled to jump up from the dinner table and wash the dishes as soon as the meal was over. I hated doing that, but the Parent in my head (my dead stepmother) drove me. She insisted this was the right way, the only way. When I groaned about my martyrdom (a favorite trick of compulsive people—expecting praise for being "good" and eternally disappointed), Bernie was surprised. "What's your hurry," was his mild retort. "The dishes will wait. Relax."

This was a new angle and I examined it for some time before I dared to experiment, to see how much punishment I might have to take from the Parent in my head if I dared to assert my independence. The first few times I was a little uneasy sitting around chatting or reading while dirty dishes clamored for attention. But I continued to *discipline* myself to resist that pressure and little by little the discomfort evaporated. Finally the day came when I discovered to my surprise that if I wait until I am good and ready to wash dishes, that chore is not boring but actually satisfying. I always hated chores performed under my stepmother's direction, but now, functioning on an Adult level, I can enjoy washing dishes.

Years ago, when I was planning to write my first book, I told Bernie I was afraid I would never find time to fit an hour's writing into my busy day. He suggested I cut down on something to make time. "Cut down on what?" Everything seemed so essential. "How about vacuuming? You're pretty compulsive about that." I was surprised. "I am? I never knew that!"

In those days it was my custom to vacuum the entire house, all rugs and bare floors, every single day. That had been my stepmother's way and I never stopped to question it. But now I wanted to write a book so I began to experiment. At first I had to feel small doses of anxiety while I dared to disobey my stepmother. I went slowly; little by little I spaced vacuuming days further and further apart. Today I am completely free of that particular compulsion just as I am of the dish-washing syndrome. True, you can't eat off the floors in my house, but I am more fun to live with.

For years I have been reading and responding to personal journals sent by students experimenting with self therapy. It is an activity I particularly enjoy. Little by little the pile of journals has grown. About a year ago I noticed I was doing something self defeating, handling those journals in a compulsive way. Just as with writing, journal reading and correspondence is fun:

a) for a certain length of time, and
b) when I am in the mood.

If I tackle them at the wrong time or stay with them too long, the whole thing turns into homework: I am forcing myself instead of enjoying it, my teeth ache, I feel exhausted.

There is a neurotic part of me that says, "Be the Perfect Mother you never had. Don't dare go out and have fun if there are unanswered journals on your desk. You bad thing, you're neglecting your deprived children." Again, I needed to experiment with new behavior, exercise self discipline. Instead of blindly obeying that Parent voice and then sabotaging the work with fatigue and martyrdom (I call it the Jewish Mother syndrome), I am learning to pay attention to my moods. Sometimes I need to get away from people's problems for a while and turn to music or dancing or gardening, or books. I find I can let those unopened journals wait awhile. I still suffer a certain amount of guilt at such times, but I label it neurotic guilt and use it for self therapy when it becomes too painful. The Adult in me has decided that I must never read journals under circumstances where boredom or fatigue may interfere with the pleasure of this important activity.

In the chapter, "Creativity," in SELF THERAPY, I describe my experimenting with music, art, dance, etc. I need to exercise self discipline each time I set aside a period for these activities, or for gardening. If I wait for the moment when I feel an urge to paint or play the piano or dance or dig in the garden, I will never do these things. The Parent voice reminds me of one more household chore or another unread journal waiting; the Child wants to curl up with a good book, which for me is a passive, non-creative activity, like eating —fun while it lasts, but to a compulsive reader, unfulfilling, restful but not refreshing; in a word, uncreative.

The Adult makes the decision, just as with writing an hour a day: time out for dancing a little while each morning. I never feel a conscious desire to dance unless I hear inviting music. When I am involved in my daily activities, there is no sudden craving to stop everything and have fun. But I have learned from experience that a little dancing each morning does good things for my body and mind, so at a certain time each morning the Adult starts the record player and gives the Child permission to dance. Once I get started, the Child takes over and has fun until the Adult voice says, "Back to work."

There is one area of my daily life where I would be lost without self discipline. That is self therapy. Without a conscious effort to stay with certain painful emotions— shame, guilt, inadequacy, helplessness, hurt—and let them lead me to deeper layers, I would become a robot, a kind of humanoid creature who says and does fairly reasonable things, but functions largely on a computer level, with an undercurrent of depression and mild anxiety substituting for genuine emotions, or headaches and other physical symptoms to prove I am still human.

Each time I notice myself "turning off," swallowing down something painful and thinking faster in order to cope with an unpleasant situation, I need to make a deliberate effort of will to let go of the analyzing, the intellectualizing, and let myself feel. I lean heavily on the Adult to keep the doors to feeling open when the Child acts as if she is too weak to tolerate pain and is trying to close those doors.

Some of my students tell me that once they have learned how to do self therapy, it comes easily for them. Not for me. The cold computer fights desperately to take over; the emotions have to struggle to stay alive.

6. THE JUDGMENTAL ATTITUDE

WEBSTER'S DEFINITION—*"judgment*: a formal utterance of an authoritative opinion." My own definition of the judgmental attitude includes three modes in which we function on the Parent level:

1. Disapproving, criticizing, scolding, shocked, outraged. "Your behavior is bad (stupid or crazy)." [7]

2. Condescending, teaching, helpful. "Let me teach you how to behave" (you poor stupid or crazy thing). "You are doing better, I'm glad to see." (I'll give you A for effort, you poor thing.) "I like what you did." (From my superior position I approve.)

3. Labeling, categorizing, describing his character. "You are bad, (stupid or crazy)." "You are a person I approve of" (from my superior judging position).

Acting out your judgmental feelings always creates a *barrier to communication.* It separates you from the other person, keeps him at arm's length. When you express your judgmental feelings you are playing the Parent-Child game. The other person then has a choice of four responses. He can be the obedient Child: "I'll try to do better. Help me."; the rebellious Adolescent: "Shut up, damn you. Who cares what you think?" He can out-Parent you and force you into the Child role: "How bad (stupid or crazy) of you to think you are in a position to judge me!"—or he can simply ignore you and get away as soon as possible. In any case, intimacy on a genuine peer relationship is impossible.

Acting judgmental is a way to avoid revealing our own emotions and/or a distraction to avoid feeling them. Instead of showing something of *yourself* to another ("When you did that I felt scared, hurt, angry, helpless, warm") you focus on the *other person*: you state your opinion of him. Instead of admitting *you* were hurt, you label *him* a bad, hurtful person. Instead of saying *you feel* warm and loving toward him, you hand down your judgment that *he is* a nice person, keeping your own feelings out of it. Whether you are judging him as good or bad you indicate you feel superior to him— you are one-up on him. The message he gets is that he has no power to move you, that you are merely observing his behavior from your own height.

People in families keep looking for safe, comfortable ways to act out their judgmental attitudes. Husbands and wives, parents and children complain to one another, "You won't let me be honest. I don't want to be afraid to level with you." What they really mean is, "Don't feel hurt or angry when I judge you. Don't scare me with your anger or make me feel guilty with your hurt. Just listen to my criticism and don't feel anything." This is an impossible assignment. Being judged always stirs up feelings in the victim. Communication is a two-way thing. If you do something to him, he has to do something to you in retaliation, unless he is so brow-beaten that he has to keep quiet, in which case his feelings will grow more intense.

The *danger* in acting judgmental is that you may unwittingly be talking to the other person in the same words as the cruel Parent in his own head. You may be reenforcing his own self-hatred more than you suspect or intend. He then reacts to the self-hatred you have stirred up in one of three ways: a) he may project his self-hatred on to you and punish you; b) in order to avoid feeling the self-hatred he may sink into depression; c) he may be forced to feel more self-hatred than he can safely cope with at the moment and suffer an anxiety attack or even attempt suicide.

When my older daughter was in high school she came home one day complaining about the pressure of homework assignments and term reports piling up. That evening at supper she casually mentioned she was going roller-skating with friends. In the light of her earlier conversation, I was surprised. I expressed my judgment in what I thought was a most tactful way: "I don't see how you can go out. I thought you had so much work to do." I was apalled when she snapped back, "I didn't ask you for advice!" This led to a terrible cold war between us which lasted for two silent, tortured days after which I did self therapy and was able to open the lines of communication between us. "You know I'm a hard-working student," she told me later. "Have you ever had to tell me to do my homework?" Never. She was too conscientious about school. "It's hard for me to make a decision to go out and have fun when I have any homework waiting. I have to argue with myself each time, in order to allow myself any freedom at all. When I thought you were telling me to get to work, it was too much and I flared up." We were both sorry about what had happened, apologized and forgave one another.

I had acted in a judgmental way: condescending, teaching, helpful, in an area where my daughter deserved to be treated as an adult. As a matter of fact she was a young adult, and even if she had not been so serious about her school work, the time was long past for me to talk down to her. I had unwittingly reenforced her own harsh judgment of herself and she punished me for it.

I had a similar experience when my younger daughter grew into young adulthood. In a rare moment of confidence she revealed a conflict she was facing at the time and I chose that opportunity to preach a little. That is, I carefully explained my own point of view in a last desperate effort to influence her. She responded with almost the same words her sister had used years ago. "Mommy, you've already brainwashed me. Every time I have to make a choice I ask myself, 'What would Mommy and Daddy think?'. Stop teaching me. I know all your ideas too well. I'm trying to find out what my own ideas are." Here again, instead of treating her as a peer, I was still helping, teaching, condescending as if she were a little girl, as if she needed to hear my judgments on her behavior. In both these incidents my need to teach my daughters at an age when they were obviously inner-directed, stemmed from my neurotic need to control. (See chapter, "The Need to Control")

Some grown-ups cannot tolerate children's expression of intense feelings—grief, anger, fear, jealousy, etc. Whenever you notice yourself feeling judgmental about your child's "lack of self-control," use that for self therapy. Each time you explore it you will uncover a different hidden feeling:

envy of the freedom you were cheated of long ago and which you now forbid yourself; anxiety about the intensity of his emotion which you fear is contagious—you might have to feel it yourself; the need to control and the fear of helplessness, etc.

A judgmental person may appear to be a threatening, strong Parent to the victim who has regressed to a Child level. But to the impartial observer, the judgmental person usually seems childish in his inability to tolerate individual differences and in his apparent conviction that he can and should change others. This appearance of childishness stems from the nature of his hidden feelings.

One who is chronically judgmental, for whom feeling judgmental, functioning on the Parent level, is a stereotyped reaction, is basically judgmental and unaccepting of himself. A scolding Parent voice within him constantly disapproves and criticizes almost everything he does. In order to avoid experiencing his inner struggle between the cruel Parent and the frightened Child, he directs the Parent voice *outward* toward others. As long as he can focus on other people's weaknesses he can avoid his own. As long as he scolds them, he can deafen himself to the inner self-scolding. The reason he seems childish to us is because he rarely functions on an Adult level: he swings back and forth from feeling like the judged Child (projecting his inner Parent voice on others) or the judging Parent. In the Parent role he sounds so irrational, so exaggerated, that he sounds like a small child who says to a playmate, "My Mommy says that's naughty. You're bad! *I'm* a good boy! I don't do those naughty things."

If the judgmental person becomes aware of the stereotyped pattern of his reactions, if he notices how frequently he feels like criticizing, scolding, teaching, he can begin to change. He can watch for the feeling and use it for gestalt self therapy.

Even if this is not your chronic problem, use the judgmental feeling whenever it comes along, as I do. I know that whenever I feel judgmental I am hiding something from myself. I begin with an imaginary encounter with the person toward whom I feel judgmental. Then I change one or both of us into people from my past, and eventually end by playing both sides of myself: the judge and the judged, the Parent and the Child.

The person who, at the sight of a fellow-being straying from the straight-and-narrow, flares up indignantly and self-righteously declaims the purity of his own morals, is protesting too much. Chances are he lacks strong convictions about this particular area and fears contagion. Again, like a small child, the unspoken message is, "Don't do that naughty thing. You're setting me a bad example. I want to be a good boy but I don't know what will happen if I get in bad company." Lacking inner direction, rudderless, he tries to keep others from rocking the boat in order to stay afloat himself. This is a learned attitude. Many parents habitually blame their child's playmates for leading him astray. If two children from different families are caught in forbidden behavior, each mother immediately assumes the other's child is responsible.

Feeling judgmental can serve many purposes. The judgmental person projects the scolding Parent in his head on to others and expects their disapproval. Following the principle that the best defense is a strong offense, he beats them to it by criticizing them before they can attack him.

Then there is the "sour grapes" attitude. A lonely, alienated person who wants to avoid exploring his own self-defeating behavior (which might show him his own responsibility in keeping people away), may take refuge in the judgmental stance: "You are all so bad, I don't care if I'm an outsider. I don't want to be like you," thereby pushing them further away.

For the person whose early experiences taught him to distrust others and to fear closeness, the judgmental attitude serves to ward off intimacy. He finds a variety of reasons to separate himself from his fellow beings. All kinds of human characteristics repel him. He may disapprove of a person's life style: too conforming or too off-beat; his politics: too conservative or too radical, his personal habits: too finicky or too slovenly. He sets himself up as a judge of beauty, intelligence, culture—anything that will reassure him he would be wasting his time if he allowed himself to get close to the other person. I know people who, whenever they are on the verge of falling in love, stop them-selves and suddenly begin to find fault with the lover's phys-ical appearance: his hair is too curly, he is too fat or too thin, etc.

Sometimes you feel judgmental as a cover for a hidden feeling; other times you whip up an apparent judgmental feeling and act out in order to deliberately drown out (sup-press) an emotion you have barely glimpsed and which you want to avoid feeling. In both these cases, acting out the judgmental feeling is *anti*communication: a) the other person has no idea of your true feelings and b) he tends to distort your message and exaggerate it. Acting out judgmental feelings pushes the two of you further apart instead of help-ing you know one another better.

The following are some examples taken at random from my workshops:

A says to B: "You remind me of Madame LaFarge, the woman in THE TALE OF TWO CITIES who enjoyed watching people's heads cut off by the guillotine." (*Unspoken*, delib-erately suppressed emotion: "I was hurt by what you said and I'm afraid of you now.") B suffers from a phobia about cruelty and violence with an irrational dread that he has hidden sadistic tendencies. He hears A speaking in the same words as the accusing Parent in his head and proceeds to have an anxiety attack much to the surprise and remorse of A who did not mean his criticism to be taken literally.

C says to D: "You seem like an innocent little school girl." (Unspoken message: "I am so wicked and I'm afraid if I reveal my true self to you, you will judge me and reject me.") D suffers from the obsessive conviction that she is less educated than other members and too ignorant to be accepted as part of the group (neither of which are true). She now sees C exposing her to the group, holding her up for public ridicule. She suffers depression until the following weekly meeting when she can talk about it, and discovers that C was appalled by her misinterpretation and had not meant anything of the kind.

E says to F: "You wear your hair in that tight bun be-cause you want to look cold and forbidding." (Unspoken message: "I'm angry because I think you are rejecting me." Hidden emotion: I'm frightened because I think you're rejecting me.") F's idealized self image of herself as warm and loving is in conflict with the punishing Parent in her head who insists she is bad, not loving enough. E's accusation feeds her self-hatred and pushes her into a state of depression and obsessive thinking which lasts for weeks. E is dumbfounded. He did not know that F was vulnerable in this area and had not intended to push her so hard.

G says to H in a stern, disapproving voice: "I can't understand how you can be envious of her. You should be happy for her good fortune." (Unspoken message: "I'm feeling uncomfortable and slightly anxious about this open admission of envy and I don't know why. Stop feeling envious.") H has always been ashamed of feeling envy and confessed it in fear of disapproval. Her shame is now aggravated considerably. G later discovers in self therapy that she herself is an envious person in irrational, unexpected areas. She cannot tolerate in others a trait she hates and fears in herself.

I says to J: "I don't think you should reveal such personal things in group. You shouldn't wash your dirty linen in public." (Unspoken message: "I'm embarrassed for you. I'd like to shield you from all those prying eyes." Hidden meaning: "I'm afraid I'll be tempted to act out my own compulsion to reveal painful, secret things about me.") J now feels ashamed, "like a dirty little girl."

K says to L: "You shouldn't feel that way." (Unspoken message: "I feel supportive of you. I wish you didn't have to feel painful emotions." Hidden feeling: "When you feel something painful it's a threat to me. I'm afraid it's contagious. I may be seduced into feeling painful hidden feelings of my own.") L is hurt. He thinks K is telling him he is bad, stupid or crazy and that K is not interested in hearing about his feelings.

M says to the group: "There's too much crying in this group." (Unspoken message: "You're a bunch of weaklings, letting yourselves go, indulging yourself that way." Hidden emotion: "I'm afraid to let down my defenses and feel such strong emotions. I want to get away from you—I'm afraid you'll weaken my defenses and I'll be seduced into feeling hidden, painful things.'') Some group members now feel ashamed of having revealed their inner selves in M's presence, since he speaks the words of the scolding Parents in their own heads.

N says to the group: "All this crying and display of emotion seems phony to me." (Unspoken message: "I sometimes pretend to have emotions I really don't feel. I can fool others, and I'm afraid to be fooled that way." Hidden feeling: "I'm afraid to believe you are sincere because then I'll have to feel deeply for you, empathize with you and be seduced into feeling painful hidden emotions of my own.") Some group members were hurt and others angry at N's accusation.

O says to the group: "There's too much sweetness and light here, too much warmth and loving. My problem is that I'm afraid to feel and express anger. If the group showed more anger I could let go. You're stopping me from feeling and expressing myself." (Unspoken message: 1. "I am an angry person who acts sweet and I believe you are all just like me. I can't trust your warmth so I don't feel safe enough to express my true feelings." 2. "I feel judgmental most of the time and I expect to be judged constantly by you. If you all act angry then you won't be able to criticize my anger; you will share the guilt about being bad.")

This is what I call the *"if only"* syndrome. Here are examples of the "if only" syndrome taken from my workshops:

"I'm new in this workshop. If only I weren't an outsider I could reveal myself."

"If only the kleenex box was nearer I could have let myself cry."

"If only there were fewer young people I could be myself."

"If only there were fewer older people, etc."

"If only there were more men, etc."

"If only you people didn't have such terrible problems I could try to compete."

"If only you didn't have such intense feelings, etc."

"If only you didn't discuss such trivial problems, etc."

"If only you people had the same real life problems as me, etc."

"If only we had props like other groups, I could feel anger."

"If only I knew the facts of the case I could sympathize with the person who is crying."

The "if only" syndrome is the form their resistance takes. These people go through life with the fantasy that if only the world were different, if only other people would change, they could begin to live. Unwilling to jump into a real therapeutic experience, afraid to come alive, they remain partially unborn, frittering away the precious years, waiting in vain for the magic midwife who never comes.

7. RESPONSIBILITY AND BLAME: PROBLEMS IN COMMUNICATION

THE GREATEST stumbling block to true communication is the tendency to play "lawyer." In an argument with someone close to you, as soon as you begin to recognize your desire to fix the blame ("I'm right, he's wrong. I must prove it to him,") you are headed for further frustration. You cannot handle intimate human relations from the legal angle. By the time the two of you are ready for courtroom-type arbitration your relationship has already dangerously deteriorated.

"It's not fair!" You are right: *there is no justice in human emotions.* Feelings are nonrational; the unconscious is illogical. Does the person you care about seem irrational at this moment? Then obviously you cannot reason with him now. And if you feel compelled to keep trying that is sure proof that you too are irrational, hiding something from yourself, functioning in an inappropriate, self-defeating way. [4] Justice, fairness, blame, are irrelevant issues when the other person is in the midst of an intense emotion.

Are you stuck in a close relationship with someone who has no sense of justice, who is consistently unfair and exploitative? Then work on *your* problem. Use self therapy to discover:

a) why you were drawn to him in the first place
b) what unconscious games you are playing now; how you set yourself up for exploitation, and
c) why you cannot leave him.

Remember that playing prosecuting attorney will not change him.

What happens to communication when people get involved in the legal blaming game? Here are examples taken from my workshops:

GESTALT SELF THERAPY

I. When two group members get stuck in an impasse where a) each blames the other and b) neither one can let go, it is always a two-way problem. Both people are being irrational at the same time; each is feeling pain in some vulnerable area. At such times, the question of right or wrong is irrelevant; one is not more to blame than the other. Both are right and both wrong; right in their need to feel hurt or angry or frightened because they are stirred up in a damaged area, wrong because each is over-reacting to the other, each acting out some old, unresolved problem from his own past.

II. On the other hand, suppose A is feeling irrational about something B did and blames B. If B is rational now he is able to feel and express sympathy for A's discomfort. He can show that he is genuinely sorry A distorted his statement. Often this resolves the impasse and all is well.

However, if A has too many hidden feelings at this time he distorts B's apology. If B is still rational, has nothing hidden from himself, he accepts his helplessness in the encounter and is ready to drop the whole thing and keep quiet. He is not driven to justify himself or blame A for being unreasonable.

III. But suppose A's continued irrationality stirs up some of B's hidden feelings, hits B in a sensitive area. Now B is no longer able to feel sympathetic. He too becomes irrational. The two of them then proceed to play the legal game, fighting hard to put the blame on one another. They are stuck in an impasse which stirs up feelings in other group members too.

Some people identify with A, some with B. Some, for whom the encounter has hidden meanings, find it almost unbearably frustrating and want to see it settled immediately. Others cover their anxiety with boredom. Those for whom this problem has no hidden meanings can see both sides and sympathize with both. They can tolerate the impasse and listen absorbed, fascinated, no matter how long the struggle goes on.

The need to blame stems from the fear of being blamed.

RESPONSIBILITY AND BLAME

People who are always blaming others, for whom blaming is a stereotyped reaction, are trying to avoid feeling their chronic inner conflict between the blaming Parent and the frightened Child. Sometimes they project the Parent on others: they think others are blaming them. Sometimes they project the Child on others and themselves act out the blaming Parent.

Blaming is a system of *avoiding responsibility*. Sometimes the responsibility is real, as when you deliberately hurt another person. But sometimes you step on someone's toes accidentally, and then you are merely responsible for making a mistake. But if you are irrational about mistakes, if you are thinking in terms of your absolute perfection or your utter worthlessness, you resent anyone calling attention to your error. It seems to you that if you accept *any responsibility at all*, you are accepting blame. You feel compelled to fight hard to avoid being judged guilty. The weapon you use is blame, accusing someone else.

IV. A misinterprets something B says and feels hurt. B has no hidden feelings about this, is rational at the moment. He does not feel blamed by A; he simply translates A's complaint to mean; "Ouch, that hurts!" so he is able to tell A, "I'm sorry you were hurt. That's not what I meant at all. I only meant . . . etc," and clears up the misunderstanding. B is willing to accept responsibility for accidentally hurting A.

V. On the other hand, C misinterprets D's words and he too reacts inappropriately with hurt. D has hidden feelings about this situation, and so he resents C's complaint, and says accusingly, "You're trying to make me feel guilty." D blames C for blaming him, although C was not thinking about blame, only saying "Ouch!" D did not deliberately, consciously set out to hurt C, but he is afraid to accept any responsibility for accidentally hurting C and so he hurts him more by withholding sympathy and by blaming C for daring to complain.

VI. E speaks in a punishing way to F and F shows he is hurt. If E is now feeling rational he admits that he was angry and that he struck out with cruel words. He accepts responsibility for his actions and does not blame F for complaining.

VII. If F, instead of acting hurt, scolds and blames E for punishing him, E responds with counter-blame. He either justifies his original position, or insists that F is really the punishing one. Then they are stuck in the impasse described in I above.

VIII. G is angry and hurts H. H expresses hurt and G blames him: "You're trying to make me feel guilty." G is afraid to accept responsibility for his actions and he resents H's complaint which sounds like blame to him. People with a great deal of hidden guilt tend to project their own self-blaming on others. They think others are blaming them, trying to make them feel guilty. Suppose someone is actually trying to make you feel guilty. If you have no hidden guilt in this particular area, you will not be upset. You will not blame him for blaming you.

IX. J is angry at something K said to him. K does not respond to J's feelings, does not say, "I'm sorry I made you angry." Instead, he justifies himself and blames J. K: "You don't understand. Let me explain. You shouldn't feel angry." The unspoken message is "Don't blame me for your feelings. It's all your fault for misunderstanding me." This further angers J.

X. M reacts inappropriately to L's behavior. L is afraid to accept responsibility for accidentally bumping into M's vulnerable area, so he blames M for complaining. L: "Don't blame me if you're irrational. That's your problem." He cannot respond to M's feelings.

Whenever we play the legal, blaming game we are incapable of feeling sympathy, empathy or warmth. These emotions play little part in legal action.

Here are some ways people use blame to avoid responsibility:

"Our marriage would be fine, we would be a happy family if it weren't for this problem child." The parents are using the child as a scapegoat, avoiding responsibility for providing a family atmosphere where a child develops serious problems. Family therapists discover that when the identified patient gets better the parents' marriage often deteriorates. [7]

"My husband doesn't want me to go to church [or therapy, or workshops, or have friends, or pursue my own interests]. I'm so deprived. It's all his fault." Some married people blame their partners for their own inertia and lack of courage. They avoid responsibility for their own lives.

"My wife won't discipline the kids," "My husband won't give them enough attention." Focusing on the other's shortcomings can serve to avoid exploring your own strengths and weaknesses, your own responsibility to make up for his lack.

In psychotherapy we learn to feel residues from the past, old anger, hurt and frustration toward our parents. These feelings should be used as steppingstones to growth. Some patients hang on to blame in order to avoid responsibility for change: "I can't help being angry with my wife when she does that. It's exactly what my mother used to do." This man is misusing his new-found self-knowledge to justify old patterns rather than using it as material for change.

Here are revealing comments heard in my workshops:

"I know people don't like me because I'm just born unloveable. I'm not attractive [or charming, or intelligent] enough. It's my fate to be lonely." This person refuses to take responsibility for his actions. When group members give him negative feedback, explaining in simple, concrete terms exactly what he is doing that irritates them, he refuses to take them seriously. Instead of using this valuable information about his self-defeating behavior for self therapy and trying to change, he chooses to ignore it and stick with his fantasy that they dislike him for some mysterious reason over which he has no control.

"I always have bad luck. Everything happens to me." Our earliest experiences simply happened to us: we were once helpless and at the mercy of others. But blaming fate or other people continually in adult life for present bad experiences is a way to avoid responsibility for self-defeating behavior. You have freedom to make new and better experiences for yourself as you develop new self-awareness and experiment with new patterns of behavior.

"I can't stand you because you remind me of my father. Sorry about that." (It's my father's fault and there's nothing I can do about it.) "It's nothing personal. Don't feel bad." (I am not responsible for feeling or saying this and so you have no right to be hurt or angry.) It is irresponsible to act out a feeling toward someone which you know is irrational and inappropriate unless you go further and explore its hidden meaning. When you work it through in gestalt self therapy your bad feeling about this present person changes. You begin to see him as himself, not as a mere shadow from your past. It is your responsibility to yourself and others to try to separate the past from the present.

"He won't give me the right to express my opinions." No one can *give* you that right: you must take it yourself. Blaming someone else for withholding permission to be honest is avoiding responsibility for your own actions. You are blaming him for reacting to your words with his own feelings —hurt or anger or fear. You are demanding the privilege of acting out without assuming responsibility for the effect of your behavior on him. You want a guarantee that he will not react negatively to your words; you are blaming him for your own cowardliness.

A blames the group for not being more supportive of B. A himself has done nothing at all to support B and is blaming others to avoid responsibility for his own inaction.

C acts in self-defeating ways and then cannot tolerate any negative feedback from the group so she leaves the workshop prematurely. As always in such circumstances group members are troubled and discuss at length their various reactions to C's behavior. D scolds and blames the group for talking about C's shortcomings after she is gone. "You should have told her all these things while she was here, so she could learn from it." But D has been the most cautious person in the group. She was overly careful of C and too protective of her: she intervened and scolded another member when he attempted to be honest with C. D is blaming the group in order to avoid her own failure in responsibility toward C.

E: "There's too much trivia expressed in this group. I don't hear any deep feelings expressed." As a matter of fact, a great many painful emotions have been experienced and shared in the group but in a low key which E cannot recognize. He himself is so out of touch with his feelings that it is difficult for him to empathize with others and he looks for some dramatic outburst to shock him out of his boredom. E has been functioning on a purely intellectual level all along. He blames the group in order to avoid responsibility for his own inability to make therapeutic use of the workshop.

Here are some useful questions to ask yourself when exploring the desire to blame or your fear of being blamed. "Who blamed whom in my past?" After you have had an imaginary encounter with the person you are blaming, try putting different people in each place.

"What is my hidden prophecy about blame? What terrible thing will I have to feel if I accept blame? Guilt? Shame? Helplessness? Self-hatred?

"Who is the judge to whom I am presenting my case?" To whom in your past are you still hoping to justify? Who misunderstood, misjudged you? In gestalt self therapy, play the judge and the accused. Then change them into the two sides of yourself.

There is a special kind of blaming and avoidance of responsibility which involves spitefulness. My stepmother was a controlling person. When she wanted to manipulate me, trick me into doing something, she would sometimes say, "Oh, you can't do that." She expected me to rise to the challenge and make a special effort to prove her wrong because she was a competitive person and could easily be motivated to try harder with that kind of challenge. But it never worked for me; it always made me stubborn. When I saw her trying to manipulate me that way I would go out of my way to prove she was right, that of course I couldn't do it. There was no room in our relationship for any overt show of my anger or frustration. Passive resistance, spite, was the only weapon I had to maintain my self respect.

Some people act out their spite, unaware of their motives until they uncover them in self therapy. In the chapter, "The Search for Identity," I described a compulsively *stupid* man and a c o m p u l s i v e l y *ugly* woman. Both these people go through life acting out their spite toward their parents. One pretends to be stupid and the other makes a special effort to appear ugly in order to *blame* their parents and avoid *responsibility* for their own behavior. When I resisted my stepmother's attempts to challenge me to greater efforts, I could tell myself, "It's all her fault that I am failing. If she'd only leave me alone I could do very well." I could blame her for my self-defeating behavior.

I believe that this kind of spiteful behavior is a fairly good choice for a child under such circumstances. It helps him maintain his personal integrity. When you have no weapon left but spite, you have to use it to stay sane. The tragedy is that some of us never let go of that weapon. We continue to use it years after the need for it has disappeared. As I write this now it occurs to me for the first time that one facet of my writing block stems from spite. I used to get rave reviews from English teachers for my compositions at school. One particularly effusive teacher told me she expected the Great American Novel from me some day. Each time I repeated this kind of compliment to my stepmother she would immediately deflate me "for my own good." Her favorite verdict was, "Of course you have the gift of gab, you are very glib. But you have nothing original to say, so you'll never be a creative writer." I haven't worked it through in self therapy yet, so this is only an educated guess, but I think one reason I cannot work on this book for more than an hour a day, one reason I cannot think of myself as a writer, is my spiteful attitude toward my stepmother. Perhaps I am still resisting her negative challenge, still saying, "Yes, you are so right. I can't write."

Every neurotic tendency is over-determined. That is, it has many causes. The spiteful, rebellious Adolescent, the frightened Child, the punishing Parent have accummulated from a history of painful experiences. They all combine to push us into self-defeating behavior.

8. THE NEUROTIC NEED TO CONTROL

THE NEED to control is the most common of all neurotic traits. The control-mad person tries to blueprint his life in order to avoid surprises. Unlike the healthy man (who is curious about the unknown), the *controller* fears the unpredictable. He wants to program people and events. When the other fellow's thoughts and feelings are different from his own he is intolerant and contemptuous. Underneath this apparent contempt lies hidden fear. The controlling person feels threatened by autonomous, self-directed people even when they feel kindly toward him: their spontaneity makes them unpredictable. He tries constantly to control other's feelings toward him, but even when their attitudes are exactly what he has longed for, he cannot be satisfied. Because he overestimates his ability to control them, he cannot believe their feelings are genuine. To him they are merely puppets. A puppet-master in a world of puppets is a lonely creature.

Whenever you are driven by the need to control others, you use one or more of three weapons: anger, blackmail and manipulation.

You use *anger* as a weapon when you act out intense, dramatic anger or when you threaten to withdraw love or security. This is most effective when the victim is dependent on you, as in a parent-child relationship. This relationship may be either biological or psychological as in marriage, friendship, love or psychotherapy.

You *blackmail* when you force the other person to feel pity or guilt: "You're giving me a headache." "You're breaking my heart!" "I'm having a heart attack." "I'm going to kill myself." This method gradually becomes ineffective with prolonged use on the same person.

You can *manipulate* by appeasing, seducing, brain-washing, playing Parent or Child.

Appeasing: "I didn't really mean it. Can't you take a joke?" "I'm so sorry. I didn't mean to hurt you. I take it back." "Don't feel bad. I really like you."

Non-sexual seduction: Enlist him on your side. "I like you. No matter what you do I'll always defend you" (and I expect you to reciprocate).

Sexual seduction: If you have a hidden fear of members of the opposite sex you can render them harmless by flirtation or overt sexual relations.

Brain-washing: Drown him in a barrage of arguments and intellectual discussion until he cannot think clearly.

Playing Parent: "Let me help you, teach you, protect you. Lean on me."

Playing Child: "You're so clever, tell me what to do. . . . Yes, but I can't do that. Save me, help me . . . Yes, but . . . etc. etc." If you choose someone with a neurotic need to play Parent you can hold his attention for years.

THE PERSON WHO CONTROLS HIMSELF

These people fall into two main categories.

1. Some neurotics try to control people by controlling their own emotions, functioning like computers on a purely intellectual level. This *turned-off* person is more frightened of his own feelings than of other people's. His unconscious fantasy is that the hidden material, if allowed to escape, would overwhelm him, force him to act out in destructive ways, stir up others to terrible reactions, and in general create havoc in the world. His goal in life is to maintain order in the face of potential chaos. He exercises constant vigilance over his own and others' emotions. His monotonous voice, immobile face and rigid posture gives an impression of deadness. Sometimes, with the use of liquor or drugs, he actually experiences his terrible alienation from himself and his fellow-men. If he dares to feel it often enough in self therapy (without chemical aid), he can begin to change: the statue can come alive.

2. Another type of neurotic who is almost completely out of touch with his real feelings is what psychiatry calls the *hysteric.* Like the turned-off person described above, he too is alienated from his true self. In order to avoid feeling the resultant deadness, however, the hysteric seizes on slight passing apparent emotions and whips them up to something impressive. Mild irritation is expressed with shouts of rage; anger is displayed in temper tantrums; fleeting sympathy with protestations of love; faint disapproval in words and tone of utter contempt; momentary sadness in words and bodily stance of heartrending grief.

This system (whipping up apparent emotions) serves several purposes:

a) It wards off deadness and chronic depression.
b) It serves as a cover for and distraction from genuine, hidden emotions.
c) It controls other people's feelings. It stirs them up to sympathy, fear, love, anger, etc. at will.
d) It fools the public: it gives the impression that he, the hysteric, is more sensitive, capable of deeper feelings than other "ordinary" people.
e) He fools himself: imagines himself more sensitive, etc. than others.

From time to time the heavy back-log of hidden feelings seeps out in the form of anxiety attacks or deep depression.

The person who controls others by controlling his own real feelings in either of these two ways, 1) by deadening himself, or 2) by whipping up apparent emotions, tends to project his control-madness on to others. He thinks everybody else is just like him. Underneath his need to control is the dread of being controlled by others. He is afraid that if he dares to simply feel whatever comes along, if he relaxes vigilance for a moment, the other person will gain control over him. The craving for power comes from the hidden fear of helplessness, of being controlled.

These two people, the turned-off one and the hysteric, gravitate toward one another and tend to form long-term emotional partnerships. Since their life-styles are apparently so different, neither one recognizes that they are basically identical, that both of them fear being controlled, want to control others, and are out of touch with their own feelings.

The hysteric, on an apparent, verbal level keeps encouraging the turned-off partner to come alive, to feel and express emotions.

The hidden message is, "Feel *what I want* you to feel, *when I want* you to." He attempts to control his partner's feelings with every tool available: "You cold fish, I'll leave you." "You're breaking my heart with your insensitivity." "I feel so sorry for you, you poor neurotic. Let me help you get closer to your feelings."

Since the turned-off person is terrified of being controlled, constantly on guard, these controlling tactics force him to dig in his heels and turn himself off more than ever.

Neither partner ever seems to notice that the hysteric contradicts himself, that he acts exactly opposite to his avowed intention to free the turned-off one from his deadness. On the rare occasion when the turned-off person dares spontaneously to feel and express a genuine emotion of his own, not directed by the hysteric, he is punished with fear, blackmail, or manipulation. If the turned-off one exercises anger, the hysteric accuses him of inhuman cruelty; if he shows warmth toward another person the hysteric acts out irrational jealousy; if he demonstrates weakness the hysteric feels contempt. The turned-off one promptly goes back to his shell and the hysteric continues to nag him about his coldness.

The turned-off person is at first fascinated by the lifestyle of the hysteric and draws closer in order to warm his hands at this fire. Then he spends the rest of his life pouring cold water on it ("Sh-sh-sh! Don't get so excited. Don't cry. Calm down. There's nothing to get so excited about. You're embarrassing me. I'm bored, etc."). Besides, he is so stubbornly resistant to any attempt to stir him up, that the hysteric is driven to greater and more fantastic heights of drama in a vain hope of getting some reaction, much as an actor will try harder to wake up a dead audience. So the turned-off person also gives a double message. He says, "Change your style. Be more like me, restrained," but his deliberate lack of response stimulates the hysteric to more brilliant fireworks.

RESULTS OF CONTROLLING

Controlling behavior, like any neurotic pattern, is always self-defeating. The Child within the controlling person is hungry for love and security. But puppets cannot feed the puppet-master; you are condemned to starvation as long as you depend on such artificial nourishment. Even if you manage to frighten, blackmail or manipulate people into responding in accordance to your desires, the Child within will mistrust their responses and grow more ravenous.

The control-mad neurotic tends to form a relationship with one who is peculiarly resistant to control. The two then live in a state of chronic mutual frustration.

Playing the role of Parent—teaching, preaching, advising, scolding—often strengthens an existing Parent voice in your victim's own head. He then projects that inner scolding voice on you and escapes his own conflict about obesity, laziness, alcohol, drugs, or whatever problem you think you can help him solve. When you are parental and controlling you push him into the Rebellious Adolescent role and that slows up his progress; it lessens his chances of facing his inner conflicts and resolving them. Your behavior is self-defeating: it accomplishes the opposite of your "good" intentions. Incidentally, you are ruining any chance of a peer relationship with him.

Some people hope to grow healthy by imitating healthy people, trying to hypnotize themselves into feeling "healthy" emotions. By all means try to avoid acting out irrational attitudes, but remember to let yourself *feel* whatever comes along. The healthy person is our model in terms of goals, but there is no short cut to growth. If you attempt to control your "bad" feelings and force the "good" ones, you are simply adding new neurotic defenses to the old. Do you want to stop feeling jealousy, fear, rage, intolerance? If you control these emotions, cover them up with apparent sweetness and light, you will eventually develop new symptoms: depression, anxiety, psychosomatic illnesses. You don't cure an infection by covering it up, only by letting the poisons come out. Underneath the "bad" feelings are "good" ones— warmth, compassion, empathy, strength. The path to health is an inward journey, through all the accumulated layers of a lifetime.

CURING THE NEED TO CONTROL

How can you recognize yourself as a controlling person? Watch for these frequently recurring reactions:

a) You cannot tolerate daily events; you think obsessively about changing them.
b) You cannot tolerate others' thoughts, feelings, actions; you think obsessively about changing them.
c) You are repelled by details in others: physical appearance, their dress, talk, laugh, etc. You are judgmental about others' life style: too reactionary or too conforming or too off-beat; too fastidious or too slovenly; too *different from you.*
d) You feel compulsively responsible for changing events and people, you suffer intense disappointment, frustration, obsessive thinking or anxiety when you fail.

Now you have something to work with. Use these symptoms—frustration, disappointment, obsessive thinking, anxiety—for the first of four stages as described in the chapter, "The Search for Identity", and listed here:

I. Self therapy on self-defeating behavior.
II. Look forward to similar experiences.
III. Gestalt self therapy on inner conflict.
IV. Some small change in behavior.

An example is my neurotic attempt to control my students' growth. I am a teacher of self therapy. That is my conscious and declared goal. Despite some of my students' tendency to see me as a Wise Old Woman with magic answers, I know that when they are in touch with their true feelings and thinking rationally they are perfectly capable of solving their own problems. I know my job is simply to teach them ways to reach their feelings so they can think clearly. But every once in a while I find myself tempted to assume more responsibility for someone than is reasonable.

I once found myself thinking obsessively about a student whom I will call Loretta. During leisure moments I would compulsively rehearse arguments and lectures designed to break through her stubborn resistance. Conferences were degenerating into debate. Each left me tense with frustration. Today I know that obsessive thinking and frustration about a student always indicate I am hiding something from myself and that I need to do self therapy. In those days, less self aware, I acted out the fantasy that if I worked harder I could solve this fascinating problem: Loretta's declared wish to improve her marriage and her continual pleading for help, versus her unrelenting sabotage of any suggestion—"Yes, but . . ." (see non-sexual seduction described earlier in this chapter).

Finally, when the obsession began to trouble my sleep and Loretta was haunting my dreams I recognized it must have hidden meanings and that I should use it for self therapy. That was Stage I.

I explored my attitude toward Loretta and let myself feel my desperate need to save her marriage. When I asked myself, "What does this remind me of?" (Appendix I) I was able to cry about my own parents' separation and the loss of my five-year-old world.

After this self therapy I realized that the Child within me was trying vainly to undo the past, to save my parents' marriage, my early security, by saving Loretta's marriage. I was freed of my obsessive preoccupation and could give Loretta freedom to face her own inner conflict: her wish to save her marriage versus her wish to destroy it. I no longer needed to get in on the act. I could stop struggling with her resistance. In fact, it occurred to me for the first time that I had no way of knowing whether it was better for the marriage to be saved or destroyed!

Stage II. Look forward to similar experiences. After that, with new self-awareness, I could observe my neurotic tendency to try and save marriages. Whenever the temptation arose I could use self therapy to recognize the wish to control, to remember the helpless Child who failed to save her parents' marriage and I could *let go*. I could limit myself to teaching that student to know himself and let him eventually make his own decision about his marriage.

Now that I was conscious of my need to control, I could see other similar danger zones. Whenever I found myself thinking obsessively about a student, rehearsing ways and means of teaching him, frustrated when he dragged his feet and sabotaged the help he asked for, I used the frustration for self therapy. Little by little, I learned that the Child within me is trying to undo the past in many ways.

The Child is trying to force parents to give their children the love, freedom, understanding and security I missed; trying to stop people from being cruel to one another as grown-ups were to me; trying to stop them from feeling frightened as I was; trying to stop them from feeling helpless as I was; trying to stop them from manipulating others as I did when I was a foster child; trying to stop them from being fooled as I was when I trusted my mother; trying to keep them from the surprise and shock I felt when my mother left me; trying to protect them from the results of their self-defeating behavior because I identify with their suffering and cannot tolerate it; trying to force them to act in rational ways before they are healthy enough to do so because I identify with their suffering and cannot tolerate it; trying to force them to work harder and get healthy faster because I identify with their suffering and cannot tolerate it.

My control-madness takes the form of an intense, obsessive desire to give this student individual instruction, to encourage him to work harder, to point out each self-defeating act and show him how to stop doing it and/or how to use it for self therapy. For a while the chosen student seems to thrive on this extra attention; he shows sudden exciting spurts of growth, but sooner or later he reacts in one or both of the following ways:

a) he resents the intensity of my teaching and sees me as a scolding Parent who cannot appreciate how hard he is working, and

b) he becomes insatiable and (like the Fisherman's Wife in the fairy tale) demands more and more of my time and effort. He accuses me of hypocrisy, of failing to fulfill an unspoken promise: a promise to be the Good Parent he dreamed of, to make him my favorite child, preferably my only child.

At this point I begin to feel sorry for myself—unappreciated, exploited. I am tormented with frustration and obsessive thinking. Whenever I am brave enough, I *use these feelings for gestalt self therapy*, Stage III. I begin with an imaginary dialogue with the student: scolding him, accusing him of ingratitude, complaining of exhaustion, begging him to let me rest, get off my back. (Like all controlling people, I act as if others have the power to control me.)

Sometimes, when I play the student begging for help, I identify with him and feel helplessness, desperate need and fear of abandonment. Then my anger changes to pity and grief about my inadequacy.

Sometimes when I play the student he is arrogant, complaining, insatiable, demanding, and I am hurt and/or angry.

Next (see chapter, "Gestalt Self Therapy") I change both of us to people from my past. Sometimes the student is my stepmother, forever disappointed in my accomplishments, criticizing, scolding, nagging me to do better, and I beg her to stop: "I'm doing the best I can. I'm so tired, GET OFF MY BACK!"

Sometimes I myself am my stepmother scolding, blaming, blackmailing the student (Little Muriel) with guilt, threatening her with rejection.

Sometimes the student is Little Muriel begging Big Muriel to rescue her, to undo the past and Big Muriel feels helpless and begs for forgiveness.

Sometimes the student is Little Muriel accusing me of being depriving, rejecting, selfish just like my mother and I feel guilt and self-hatred.

Eventually, I end by playing the two sides of myself, Soft Muriel and Tough Muriel. Soft Muriel longs for magic power to undo the student's past, to fulfill all his needs, to make him happy. Tough Muriel sneers at Soft Muriel ("You want to feel like a saint, you phony! Who the hell do you think you are?") yells at her, and pounds the couch furiously. "Let go, damn you!'' she screams. ''Let people do their own work. Stop smothering them.'' And all the while Soft Muriel is crying bitterly, wanting desperately to accomplish the imimpossible.

At this time of my life, both sides seem equally matched. The yelling and hitting is exactly as intense as the crying. But each time I do gestalt self therapy, each time I consciously experience that inner conflict, the Adult grows stronger; I can solve the immediate problem in a rational way, I can make some small change in my neurotic pattern, I can transcend my neurosis for the time being. As I look back over the past few years, I see how much less controlling I am now, how much more willing to let go, to allow people opportunities to move at their own pace which is what self therapy is all about.

SOME SIMPLE THERAPEUTIC EXERCISES
FOR CONTROLLERS

Try holding your breath with your face down under water and let every muscle in your body relax. Don't stretch out, don't try to float on top of the water; just act as if you were dead and let go. The first time I tried this, I was frightened. I had never really let go before. After a while I found it the most restful experience imaginable. This is useful even in a pool, but in a tropical ocean, with mild waves pushing you around, it is a most therapeutic experience for a controlling person, as I discovered on vacation in Hawaii.

Let yourself cry any place, any time, even if you are not sure why you are crying. I have embarrassed waiters in every restaurant in town crying with friends at lunch. My public image is less important to me than my mental health.

Notice when you are about to rush into impulsive action to avoid anxiety. Postpone the decision and stay with the anxiety as long as possible. Eventually you will be able to use it for self therapy.

Whenever you feel frustrated, tense or angry, hit a pillow or cardboard box and yell.

Relax in a warm bath.

THE NEED TO CONTROL

Dance in a wild, abandoned fashion.
These last two exercises are part of my daily routine!

9. THE COURAGE TO FAIL

WE LIVE in a success-ridden society and so we tend to think that fear of failure is an inborn human trait. But the craving to excel is not universal. Some cultures have a different viewpoint. Anthropologist Ruth Benedict writes about the Plains Indians to whom competition, outstripping one's peers, is shameful.

Our preoccupation with success distorts our values and can warp our lives. Erich Fromm [28] calls ours a "marketing society". Modern man focuses on his market value, his public image, at the expense of personal identity. Abraham Maslow [9] says we experience ourselves as *things* with no intrinsic worth outside our exchange value. Arthur Miller's play, "Death of a Salesman", portrays this kind of tragedy.

David Ausubel [29] believes the obsessive craving for success stems from a basic lack of self-esteem. He describes the parent who over-evaluates a special facet of a child's personality—talent, intelligence, beauty, charm, etc.; the parent who sees his child as a mere extension of his own personality, a status symbol, something to show off. This child is never accepted and loved for his whole self so he never develops genuine self esteem, All his life he will be driven by a neurotic craving for success, insatiable for more and more praise, which is the closest thing to love he has known. This is the "over-achiever", one who, through enormously hard work and single-mindedness, accomplishes more than might be expected from the basic quality of his talent and intelligence. Tragically, no amount of success ever gives him the self-esteem he craves.

David Riesman [15] believes that the need to succeed was an earlier, traditional American value belonging to the "inner-directed" man and that it has given way to the new craving for popularity of the "other-directed" man.

I think we have a painful mixture of the two drives. I see

them existing together in conflict: the need to succeed in personal accomplishment *plus* the need to succeed in popularity. In Victorian times it was enough to climb higher by stepping on your fellowmen; you could proclaim yourself a success. Today, to win friends and influence people is just as important a goal as personal achievement. You need to get ahead by elbowing others out of the way, but you must find a way to do it *without their knowing it*. You cannot openly grab what you want from others: you will not feel successful if they resent you. You must learn to manipulate them, grab so subtly that they do not feel deprived. They must admire you for your success and like you.

The truly healthy man (Maslow's model for growth) transcends his environment. He sets himself goals beyond the possibility of achievement, goals not dictated by his culture's definition of success or failure. The true artist, unmoved by public acclaim or rejection, works constantly toward his ideal of perfection.

Unfortunately, most of us are contaminated by society's standards. We struggle all our lives to avoid the stigma of failure as if surrounded continually by judge and jury. Some of us protest, "But I don't care about getting rich! Money is not that important to me." But what about other kinds of success? Each little subculture has its own measurements of status: academic, social, artistic, political. There are many kinds of success besides financial.

I know people whose attitude toward reading has been poisoned by their parents' obsession with academic success. As children they were seduced by excessive praise and excitement about good grades in school. The reading process became contaminated by the drive for success. Now they are unable to enjoy reading for pleasure. The printed page has become a means to an end, an assignment. They are deprived of the joys of reading for fun, like people who cannot relish the taste of food but simply eat to stay alive.

I was a foster child and missed the loving concern of proud parents when I was learning to read. Nobody cared whether I could read or not. I was lucky: a good book today is just as enchanting as the first fairy tales that held me enthralled so long ago.

GESTALT SELF THERAPY

Success can have a hidden meaning which drives us to self-defeating behavior. Joyce was a young woman who complained bitterly because her husband spent so little time at home. His inordinate ambition kept him working long hours. "Barry made up his mind that by the time he's 30 he must be worth—" here she named a considerable sum of money. "I'm proud of his ambition and I do everything to encourage it, but I'm worried about our marriage. We never got a chance to know one another. And I'm worried about little Jamie. He hardly ever gets to see his Daddy and he's getting awfully hard for me to handle. I'm so nervous and cranky these days, I know I'm not a good mother." Joyce began to explore her own hidden reasons for encouraging Barry's ambition. She recalled the misery of college days in a sorority chosen by her social-climbing mother, where she always felt out of place among richer girls. Little by little she learned how her mother's values had contributed to her own feelings of inadequacy. Joyce finally saw her fantasy that Barry's worldly success would magically change her self image, give her the poise and certainty she lacked, as just a fantasy. She came to understand she could not afford to deprive her child and herself of needed companionship in exchange for an irrational dream.

Marjory was a charming, likeable girl, the most popular of all the young married set in the neighborhood. Now her husband was getting a job promotion and they would move to another state. Marjory was depressed for the first time in life and could not understand why. She knew it had something to do with moving, but what? She was not afraid of strangers. She did not expect loneliness or rejection: she trusted her proven ability to make friends easily. What could be troubling her? Finally, in self therapy, she uncovered the hidden feeling—fear of failure. Marjory had always striven for popularity and never failed to achieve her goal. Her self image, her sense of identity, was bound up with her role of most popular girl in the crowd. What if she failed in this new venture? Maybe people in the new town would not be charmed by her. This hidden fear of failure (hidden because she was ashamed to know this about herself) brought on her depression. When she dared to feel it, the depression disappeared.

The actress, Marilyn Monroe, was once a love-starved child. She worked hard to become a world sex symbol with an aura of childlike innocence. I think the unconscious drive behind her ambition was the fantasy that if she could make the whole world love her, the starved Child within her would be satisfied. I believe that when she finally achieved success she recognized the fallacy of that fantasy and then there was nothing left to live for. Others too have been known to commit suicide at the height of their careers; people who worked all their lives to achieve some worldly success which had hidden meanings for them, who threw it all away when they realized that success has no magic power to undo the past.

The hidden meaning of success may be dangerous, may push a person into self-defeating patterns.

At a social gathering the conversation turned to Sunday painters, people who do not consider themselves professional artists, but paint just for fun, in their spare time. One young woman shrugged off the whole idea: "Oh, I couldn't bear to waste a year of my life painting and then discover I had no talent!" Success was her only justification for creative expression. (See chapter, "Creativity", in SELF THERAPY.) To discover lack of talent, to experience failure, was too dangerous.

Mary is gifted in writing, painting and music. She grew up under the shadow of an authoritarian father with rigid ideas who despised mediocrity. "If you cannot be a concert pianist," he warned her, "you should not play the piano." He brain-washed Mary so thoroughly that she never allows herself to pursue any of her talents. How can she be absolutely certain to write a successful novel, paint a masterpiece or perform in concert? There are troubled times in her life when she desperately needs the therapeutic value of creative outlets, but Father (although long dead, still in her head), forbids her to experiment.

John has two talents, writing and painting. From time to time he dabbles in each, takes a course or two, works up tremendous excitement, but never completes a project. He has never finished a promising picture or fascinating story. Creativity for John is contaminated with fantasies of success. "I'm a failure," he told me. "I've failed in my career and I've failed in love. I can't hold a job or a woman. I'm so sick and tired of pity. Whenever I begin a painting or a story and I feel that creative power in me, I get terribly excited. I think, what if this turns out to be a marvelous picture or the great American novel! Then they'll see who I really am. I'll show them!"

These fantasies of success block John's creative attempts. He cannot pursue his work in the arts because his hidden fear is, "Suppose, when it's finished, it is *not* a success?" As long as he never completes any project he need never face failure.

Cynthia is a dancer, but, as she frequently protests, only as an amateur. She began to be aware of her peculiar reaction to compliments on her dancing. She always felt a twinge of resentment toward people who praised her. Self therapy uncovered the hidden meaning.

Cynthia loved her silent, withdrawn father and when she was a little girl she longed for understanding and personal recognition from him. She used to write poetry in those days, and when she timidly showed her work to her father he often praised it. He was proud of her talent and encouraged her to improve the poem, giving her advice on the mechanics of it. But he never seemed to care about the content, the meaning of the poem, just as he never paid any attention to her feelings or ideas. He could appreciate the technique but not the essential Cynthia. In self therapy she was able to let herself feel the deep, unfulfilled longing for something more from him, something deeper than praise for success in artistic endeavor. Then she realized that present day compliments stirred up the deprived Child within.

A study was made of underachieving boys, youngsters whose school work falls far below their actual potential. Results showed that most of these children have fathers who are labelled failures. The hidden meaning of the boys' failure is fear of competing with their fathers. Success is too dangerous for them. The mother who criticizes and downgrades her husband, hoping to inspire her son to greater efforts ("Don't be a failure like your father!") is self-defeating.

We have learned to be ashamed of failure and are haunted by that shame. The average "well-adjusted" person (a far cry from Maslow's "healthy" man) lives in dread of a real or imagined audience and/or the scolding Parent in his head waiting to sneer as soon as he slips and falls. One false move and all is lost.

In my workshops I notice how people flinch when they hear the word "pity". They feel degraded, not supported; judged, not comforted. I watch others struggling to find tactful words of sympathy, trying to protect the other person against his own foolish pride. Shame is another name for pride; fear of failure is false pride.

This phobic attitude toward failure distracts us from our deeper feelings, keeps us from growing. Adversity, pain, can be therapeutic only when we dare to experience our true emotions. To fail from time to time in work, love, friendship, parenthood, is part of the human condition. When we stumble and fall and pick ourselves up again we learn to know and accept ourselves. This kind of self awareness brings us closer to others, more accepting of their weaknesses: it makes us more human.

But when we focus on the *shame of failure* we are warding off feelings that enrich us; we dehumanize ourselves. The only way we can avoid painful feelings is to cover them up, push them down where they will add to and aggravate earlier hidden emotions, make us more neurotic.

If we peel away the layer of shame and feel what lies underneath, if we stop focusing on the problem of success and failure, and experience all the emotions stirred up by this misfortune, we can take a big step forward in our personal growth.

Example: Mabel is jilted. Her sweetheart falls in love with somebody else. If, at this time, Mabel narrows herself down to the area of success and failure, pride and shame, she limits herself to the following reactions:

a. Shame in the presence of an audience. Obsessive thinking about what "they" are saying about her. Imagining how "they" are pitying, sneering, laughing at her because she failed.

b. Shame in the presence of the Parent in her head. The Parent says, "You are a failure. You can't hold a man." The Child says, "Yes, I know. I'm worthless."

c. Pride and self deception. The Rebellious Adolescent fights the judgmental Parent, "Well, I'm glad I found out what he's like. He's just not worth crying about. He's not good enough for me. Who cares?"

This kind of thinking keeps Mabel from feeling too much pain just now. The hidden feelings will fester and return some day in disguised form when she is less able to understand and cope with them.

If Mabel can get past the culturally-imposed obsession with success and failure, pride and shame, go into her deeper emotions and use them for self therapy, she may be able to feel:

a. Bereaved. Freud said long ago that it is natural and *necessary* to go through a mourning period when you lose a loved one. If Mabel permits herself to suffer this loss now it will not rise up later to haunt her in the form of depression.

b. Helpless. Mabel lost her father when she was small. She can use this present loss to work through some of that earlier trauma now.

c. Frightened, surprised. Still stuck at that childhood level of her father's desertion, she has been unrealistic and naive about human relationships. If she explores the shock of that earlier surprise, she will grow, become more aware of reality, less self-defeating.

d. Jealous. Her mother always seemed to prefer her sister to Mabel. If she can use this jealousy of the other woman as a door to the past, it may bring her closer to her sister.

If she dares to experience and explore these feelings instead of hiding them from herself, she will look back some day and realize that she has grown from this painful experience.

The most creative way to treat shame and fear of failure is to recognize it as a culturally-derived, apparent emotion, the first step in self therapy, and try to discover what it is hiding. Years ago I used to teach self therapy three nights a week in three different Adult Schools. I had a good following in two communities but the third never quite caught on. Each term the registration for that school just barely reached the requisite number. Whenever the attendance fell below a certain minimum the principal threatened to drop the course. This fate hung over me like a dark cloud and I began to dread each session. One winter evening, in the midst of a flu epidemic when many students were absent, the principal delivered his usual dire warning in terms of an ultimatum. It looked like the beginning of the end.

Driving home after class I felt depressed. That was Step 1, recognize a painful or inappropriate emotion. Step 2, what was I feeling? Shame; I was losing a class: I had failed. Step 3, what did I feel before this shame, during all those weeks of insecurity? An obsessive need to reach those people, to teach them. A compulsion to hold on to this class as if something terrible would happen if they lost me and my precious message. Step 4, what does this remind me of? There it was, my lifelong preoccupation with communication. I had come to it many times in self therapy—the craving to communicate and the dread of being stopped. The hidden feeling was anxiety.

I let myself feel the anxiety, the fear of an unknown catastrophe: something terrible would happen if I could not communicate. Then, in a moment or two, the anxiety was gone and so was the depression and the whole preoccupation with losing this class.

Step 5, look for the pattern. Now that I had experienced the hidden feeling and the apparent one was gone, I could lean on the Adult. (Do not call on the Adult, step 5, before feeling the hidden emotion. Your intellect can sabotage the self therapy process. As soon as the Adult steps in the Child shuts up.)

103

I could see my pattern now. Whenever my compulsive need to communicate was threatened, I suffered anxiety. It was hard for me to accept this trait in myself and I usually covered it up. This time, the conventional shame of failure was a convenient smoke screen except that I was also ashamed of being ashamed, so I tried to disguise that with depression. (I am describing this syndrome in the past tense because at this time in my life I am working hard on the whole communication hang-up and making progress. Hopefully, by the time this book is in print I will have outgrown it.)

I suddenly realized I did not want that job. I was fed up with the principal's threats, the school was too far away, three nights a week was a strain. For the first time it occured to me that any student genuinely committed to learning self therapy could follow me to either of the other schools. Actually the principal did not discontinue the course; he invited me back next term and I refused. Those students did follow me and eventually I cut out another school (see "The Office Neurosis") and lectured to one enormous class, which was more fun and less effort.

We need what David Riesman calls "the nerve of failure", the courage to fail, in order to make decisions. When you are at a cross-road in your life, you have no guarantee of success whichever direction you choose. A choice is always a gamble. The courage to change jobs, to explore latent talents, to try a new way of life rather than stay in a boring rut, to wake from lethargy and inertia—all require the courage to fail.

Love and friendship depend on the courage to fail. When you let yourself care deeply about another person, when you commit yourself to an intimate relationship, you take a chance. To face the fear of making an unwise choice, of becoming emotionally dependent, of being exploited, to chance rejection and loss, you need the courage to fail. Without this courage you condemn yourself to live in isolation.

To overcome a self-defeating pattern you need the courage to fail. Alcoholics Anonymous understand this clearly. The drunkard trying to cure himself learns to take one step at a time, to fall down and pick himself up again. "I will try to stay sober *today*," is his goal, "and if I fail, I will try again tomorrow." When the fat man goes off his diet he needs to draw on the courage to fail. Like the alcoholic, he must begin again tomorrow. The smoker trying to quit, the drug addict, the timid soul reaching out of his loneliness to others, all of us who attempt to break out of our self-made prisons need the courage to fail. Otherwise, at the first failure we label ourselves "losers" and give up.

The courage to fail means seeing yourself as truly human—a complex mixture of weakness and strength. It means fighting against the tyranny of the Idiot Child and the Cruel Parent within. One who labels himself, categorizes himself, thinks only in broad generalities, is evading this responsibility. "I'm just a born failure. Everything I touch falls apart. There's no point trying," is an admission of lack of courage to fail. As long as I don't try I can always daydream about success."

Generalizing about failure, labeling yourself, serves two purposes: a) you collect lots of sympathy from your audience, and b) you avoid concrete experiences of failure which come from actual trial and error, the real process of change and growth.

Among the painful truths I discovered as a member of an encounter group years ago, was my neurotic compulsion to make everybody like me. I discovered that to be the kind of person whom fourteen different people will love is an impossible assignment. As soon as I satisfied one who liked me passive, another preferred me when I was aggressive. When I appeared strong, some wanted me weak. When I acted weak, others despised me. My talkativeness charmed some and repelled others. I could not win. Like a rat in a maze I floundered around desperately for many sessions, but the old system would not work in this setting. I had always tried to be "all things to all men", but this was like a fast merry-go-round and I was getting dizzy.

For a while the whole problem seemed merely "real". That is, I suffered anxiety and depression trying to solve it. I did a lot of self therapy on my feelings about individual group members who disliked me, in order to cope with my helplessness. It took a long time for me to wake up to the truth, that I was simply acting out, in an exaggerated way, an old defense and that it was not working. For the first time I began to see how self-defeating my pattern was, how it slowed down my personal growth. All my life I had been so busy trying to make people love me that I dared not be spontaneous; so tactful, so appeasing, so "nice" that I was close to being a complete phony.

Where do you go with this knowledge? What do you do when you discover a pattern you do not like and want to change? You use two tools: *self therapy* and *self discipline*. I worked with both. I opened the door to all kinds of hidden meanings of this trait and, *at the same time*, I began to experiment with new behavior—spontaneity with people.

For this experiment I needed courage, the courage to fail. I still suffered from the craving for universal love and acceptance, still feared rejection. I had only begun the self therapy in this area which would need years to work through. If I dared to be my genuine self, what would happen? What if I let myself feel (and sometimes act) angry, hurt, judgmental, dangerously strong or humiliatingly weak? I was taking an awful chance: some people *might not like me*!

And of course that is precisely what happened. Some people did not like me. I failed in my neurotic quest. But I survived. I was uncomfortable for a while until the term ended, but I discovered I could live in a world where not everyone likes me. More important, I began to relish my new-found freedom to be real. It changed my whole direction; I took a giant leap forward.

One of the unexpected facets of failure is the occasional discovery that the success you once craved no longer seems important. New doors open. For years, decades, I had polished a tool I no longer wanted. I had focused on becoming a successful slave. Until I experienced freedom I could not imagine how my goals would change; that authenticity would become more precious than the talent to win friends and influence people.

Here is another case where failure opened a new door. Charles was a young man who achieved worldly success earlier than most. Suddenly, in middle age, things seemed to go wrong; money and status began to slip out of his hands. He had been at the top all those years and now he was sliding downhill. Charles was tortured by shame and fear of public opinion. In desperation he grasped at a straw: a different line of work for which he knew he had talent, one he had never fully explored before. With his customary dedication and enthusiasm he threw himself into this new field and found the work so fascinating and satisfying that, even before he knew whether or not it would pay off financially, the old failure rankled less and he was almost grateful for it. That failure gave him the opportunity to carve a new, more creative career for himself.

In order to explore our hidden feelings we need the courage to fail. The therapeutic process begins with the examination of failure. Self awareness means awareness of our self-defeating patterns, our failures. In self therapy we frequently need to let ourselves feel apparent emotions about failure—shame, guilt, inadequacy, helplessness, fear. When we look within we sometimes uncover hidden feelings of failure we have been avoiding all our lives.

For many of us, bred in a society that prizes self-reliance, the first big hurdle in seeking professional psychotherapy requires the courage to fail: to admit we need help. And in the therapeutic relationship, allowing ourselves to become dependent on another person, to form a transference, takes courage to fail. There is always some fear (sometimes apparent, sometimes hidden) that this dependency period may *not* be temporary. What if, in giving up our independence, we never regain it?

Some of us enter therapy with immediate, concrete goals in mind. Couples hope to save a crumbling marriage; parents want to "help" (control) their children; young people want to change their parents. If you are thinking of therapy as an engineering feat, a technique for managing your mind and feelings more efficiently in terms of your present standards, you need the courage to fail. Be prepared for unexpected changes. Your standards may be transformed into something very different. You may decide, when you know yourself better, that this marriage is not worth saving; that your children need more, not less, freedom from your control; that it doesn't matter if your parents cannot understand you.

The hardest feat in therapy is the leap from the conscious to the unconscious, from the apparent to the hidden feeling. It is easy to *think* about your case history, to theorize about your unconscious motivation, the origin of your neurotic patterns, but it takes courage to let yourself *feel* the secret stuff. Why is this most essential therapeutic step so difficult? Because we dread the new experience.

We turn to therapy because we dislike what we see in ourselves and we hope to get to a new place where we will like ourselves better. But we sense that the inward journey may bring us to frightening and ugly scenes. Suppose we have to hate ourselves *more* on the way? The courage to face hidden facets of ourselves, forbidden feelings, is the courage to fail. It is the courage to go deeper into the gloom with only the hope, no guarantee, that we will eventually emerge into sunshine.

It takes courage to go back to the past, to feel once again the helplessness of childhood, the horror of early traumas. You are afraid you will be trapped down there, caught forever in feelings of the past as in a time machine, that you will never come back and feel safe and strong again. Of course that is not true. The Adult is always with you. When you go back and experience an old event, you are also simultaneously here in the present. Self therapy is not the same as a psychotic break, not like insanity at all. You never lose contact with reality. It only *seems* to you that you will be completely at the mercy of whatever it was you could not afford to feel in the past. But that fear is so intense for some of us that we need courage to plunge into self therapy.

In therapy you need the courage to see how you fail to live up to your idealized self image ("Idealized Self Image" [4]). You need courage to experience your "bad" side in gestalt self therapy, to recognize and explore your projections instead of successfully rationalizing and justifying them.

When you are quivering with righteous indignation, over-reacting to the other fellow's behavior, it is sometimes a relief to ask yourself, "What does this remind me of? Who did this to me in my past?", to feel something left over from childhood and let go of the present obsession. But it takes courage to go deeper in gestalt therapy, to put yourself in the other's shoes, try his thoughts on for size. It takes courage to ask yourself, "What does this remind me of about *myself*? When have I done this same thing or wanted to do it? What do I hate in *myself* that he is reminding me of?"

When Fate seems against you, when the same terrible events keep repeating themselves again and again through the years, it takes courage to stop focusing on the "bad guys" who are mistreating you, to pay attention to your own responsibility instead of simply blaming Fate. It takes courage to face your own self-defeating behavior and discover what you are doing, what your part is in this self-fulfilling prophecy.

What about shame? ("Shame and Guilt" [4]). We can atone for guilt, but there is nothing to do with shame but feel it. This takes the courage to fail. When I began my weekly workshops I noticed that, from time to time, I would go to bed after a session feeling fine but as soon as I settled down I was wide awake, restless and slightly nauseated. I always recognized that this symptom was somehow connected with the workshop. I knew I would be forced to lie awake until I dealt with it.

So I would let my mind wander back. What happened in that workshop? What had I carefully forgotten? What was too painful to feel this evening? I had overlooked some member's significant comment or gesture or expression. Or I had intervened too soon in an encounter. Or I had spoken a careless word. Somehow I had missed the boat: wasted a precious opportunity to further the group process, to help a student learn. I had failed!

This particular kind of failure was so painful for me when it occurred that I immediately warded off my feeling about it with my own efficient defense system: my mind clicked like a computer, my tongue was smoother. I could use the mistake itself for the group's benefit: analyze it, pick up the pieces and reconstruct them into something useful and therapeutic for all. By this method I was able to salvage my self esteem and avoid feeling any discomfort about my error. I usually forgot all about it until I tried to get to sleep that night.

Bitter experience taught me I was condemned to lie awake as long as I had any unfinished business. I learned to re-live the embarrassing moment, let myself sink into the shame. I could feel myself getting hot all over for a brief while. Then the wave receded and I could sleep.

At that time I was leading four different groups each week and there were plenty of opportunities for failure. Eventually I decided to go deeper into hidden feelings about my mistakes in workshops. Suddenly the Adult popped up with a new idea. How naive and arrogant I was to be ashamed of making mistakes! Here I was, leading groups, learning as I went along. True, I had been a member of a Sensitivity Training Group and my old leader had given me his bless-ings and some guidance when he encouraged me to start on my own. True, I had faithfully studied all the material available on group process. But no-one else was conducting *Communication—Self Therapy Workshops*. This was my own invention, an experiment. I had no teacher for this. I was a novice in group leadership, attempting a brand new project, and I expected to be perfect right away, with no experience. Talk about delusions of grandeur! Who did I think I was, anyway? Some kind of genius?

Hurray for the human ability to laugh at oneself! I knew that the scolding Parent and the frightened Child within me could not hear any of this Adult logic. I could expect to feel shame again and again whenever I goofed in group. But now that I recognized how absurd my pretensions were, how ri-diculous to expect instant perfection in my role as leader, I could give myself a new assignment. From now on I would pay attention to my mistakes and try to *feel the irrational shame as soon as possible* instead of distracting myself with cleverness. I knew the longer I hid the shame from myself the longer I would be stuck in this spot. My new goal was to outgrow the shame, to accept my human fallibility in this area as I do in other areas where I am less neurotic. I had to begin with the courage to *feel the shame.*

110

THE COURAGE TO FAIL

A reward (or penalty) of personal growth is increased self awareness. Gradually more neurotic areas become glaringly obvious to you, areas that were hidden in the midst of rationalization and projection when you were too sick to see them. About once a year I am forced to see some "new" and startling stumbling block to health and then I set myself an assignment. I look for opportunities to experience that neurotic symptom whenever possible and explore it with any self therapy technique available.

For about a year at frequent intervals, I dared to face the shame of failure as group leader. In gestalt self therapy I experienced the struggle between Parent ("Shame on you, you made a mistake again!") and child ("I'm sorry. I'll try never to do it again. Stop punishing me.") I never felt *guilt* about these mistakes, only shame. (See "Shame and Guilt" [4].) I am basically a harmless person and although I have inadvertently hurt people, I have never damaged anyone. I never doubt, when I miss an opportunity to be useful to a student at this moment, that there will be many more such moments and that I can and will make it up to him.

Whenever it seemed useful to the group, I talked about my shame when I made a mistake. I began to do self therapy in their presence. Each time I came out of it, *after* I felt the shame (see chapter, "How to Use a Psychotherapist") the Adult was waiting to remind me that this shame was inappropriate, that mistakes were inevitable, that the concept of perfection itself was irrational. After about a year of hard work, I began to change.

There came a time when I noticed I had developed the courage to fail *without shame*. Today, when I say or do the wrong thing in a workshop, I can focus on the other person instead of myself. If I intervened too soon in an encounter and stopped him from expressing himself, if I reassured him too soon and blocked his feelings, I can be sorry for *him* and apologize for my error. Now that I am no longer preoccupied with my own problems I can think about *him*. The fear of failure always blinds us to others. How can we see them when shame befogs our vision? When we are obsessed with shame or pride other people are merely mirrors for our self esteem.

The inner battle still rages. When I explore other problems (i.e. the compulsion to work too hard, the craving to "save" the world) in gestalt self therapy, the Parent still demands perfection, the Child still cringes and weeps about her inadequacy. But the Adult grows steadily stronger. I am gradually becoming more accepting of my limitations and while I work hard to become a better leader, a wiser person, I am no longer tortured by my mistakes in workshops.

10. THE MEANING OF LOVE

MYTHS ABOUT romantic love feed many of our neurotic tendencies. You may enter into a love relationship with several false expectations.

a) You may think there is *one and only one* person in the world for you; that you could never be happy without him. Then, when problems arise in the relationship you "logically" conclude that you have made a terrible mistake: this was not true love after all, you must start shopping around once again for the perfect partner. This myth encourages the tendency to pass the buck, to project your inner conflicts on others and blame Fate rather than assume responsibility for your own self-defeating behavior. We are all strangers to one another and any intimate relationship requires patience, hard work and self awareness. If, like most neurotics, you have gravitated to someone whose irrational attitudes aggravate your own, a quick change of partners will not solve your problem. Without insight into your hidden feelings about him, you will "fall in love" again with someone just like him.

b) You believe that you must *successfully compete* with all rivals in everything. If he really loves you he will always see you as more beautiful (handsome) intelligent, sexy, charming, capable, feminine (virile), etc. than anyone else around. Every child at some time longs to be his parents' favorite, and the Child within you experiences your lover as Parent. The less valued you felt in childhood, the more jealous you are today. The healthy person knows he is not loved for his specific gifts, but for some indefinable something hidden in the lover's unconscious.

c) You expect him to give you *unconditional approval* at

all times; never criticize or be annoyed with anything you do. You think this blanket approval will magically supply you with the *self-acceptance* you have lacked all your life.

The small child sees himself in the mirror of his parents eyes and develops self-acceptance from their acceptance [29]. The Child within you hopes to undo the past in this new relationship and is doomed to failure. A self-accepting person is a good lover because he can easily accept the other person. If you lack self-acceptance you are intolerant of your partner's weaknesses and constantly break down his self-esteem. This makes him defensive. He is so busy protecting himself that he cannot feel in a giving mood and so he further deprives the starved Child within you. That Child is insatiable anyway and can never be sufficiently nourished from an outside source. In this case it eggs you on: you grow more demanding, more punishing, more self-defeating. You push him further away and thus further deprive the starved Child within you: a vicious circle.

d) You expect to satisfy each other better than anyone else in every area of life, not only in sex, but in intellectual stimulation and entertainment. This expectation puts a tremendous strain on a relationship. The symbiosis between infant and mother cannot safely be repeated in later life. If you live in another's pocket, you tend to lose your identity and then resent him for it. When two people depend on one another for *all* sources of pleasure and dare not have friends or pursue interests they cannot share, they eventually blame each other (either consciously or unconsciously) for their inability to find life fascinating [7]. The relationship stagnates. No lover can satisfactorily fulfill all roles of playmate, confidant, sibling and parent forever without feeling burdened and stifled.

The more each partner fulfills his *own* personality, the more he enriches the relationship. You are drawn to another because he is different from you, because he can add another dimension to your life. How wasteful to attempt to be a mirror image of one another. As the Frenchman said, "Vive la différence!"

e) You expect to approve of everything in him, never feel annoyed or critical. Only a very small child can feel this way about his parents. As you mature you develop your critical faculties and recognize that no one is perfect.

Besides, few of us are always rational. Our hidden feelings, unfinished business from the past, neurotic cravings, push us to demand the impossible. We hide our inner conflicts with symptoms like irritation, impatience, depression, anxiety, and those closest to us become our natural victims. We distort, project and blame them. If you have determined to approve of your partner at all times, never to feel anything negative about him, you have to swallow down all kinds of "bad" thoughts and feelings about him when he is being unreasonable. No matter how irrational a feeling is, even though you (hopefully) can control your overt behavior, it is dangerous to avoid feeling that emotion. If you do, you add new defenses to old, stir up more neurotic symptoms, make the work of self therapy more difficult and delay your journey toward health.

Harry Stack Sullivan said we are all more alike than we are different. Each of us has a capacity for an enormous variety of thought, feeling and behavior, but we screen out certain facets of our own personalities, channel our lives through a few narrow pathways. If you have limited yourself in this way, you will gravitate toward a person who appears to be living out the tendencies you have forbidden yourself. Putney [11] says that when that happens you tend to:

a) overevaluate his characteristics and see them as endearing and enchanting;
b) project other traits on him; imagine you see in him qualities which in fact he does not possess;
c) adore and sexualize these traits (a and b) which you would love to have yourself.

115

In other words, says Putney, you "fall in love." Putney believes that love is a neurosis.

However, my own experience and observation indicates that *a good marriage* has the following characteristics:

a) both partners are fairly self-accepting, so neither needs to degrade the other to bolster up his self-esteem.

b) they are not both neurotic about the same things. Since they are rarely irrational at the same time [4] each can tolerate a certain amount of irrational behavior from the other without over-reacting to it. Misunderstandings and differences can be tackled as problems instead of blown up to damage and eventually destroy the relationship.

c) Each is committed to the relationship, dedicated to making it work, not keeping an eye on escape hatches.

Love cannot solve all of our old problems. However, a good marriage can satisfy most of our needs for: 1) intimacy—psychological and physical; 2) sex; 3) pleasure in activities and the world; 4) self-acceptance.

1. Intimacy

a) *Psychological intimacy* between adults is like the chumship experience of the preadolescent: two people share their thoughts and feelings with one another; each makes a genuine effort to know and make himself known to the other; they empathize with one another. Psychological intimacy is a kind of coziness which helps us bear the basic existential aloneness of life. No one can truly know another, but this attempt to bridge the gap gives us comfort and strength.

b) *Physical intimacy*, separate from sex, includes all the bodily demonstrations of affection and tenderness, the animal contact that human beings need to give and receive. Some people have been so deprived and damaged in childhood that in adult life they never touch except during the sexual act. If you sexualize these needs for tenderness and simple animal warmth, you will overevaluate sex, seek it compulsively, perhaps promiscuously and be forever frustrated.

2. *Sex*. Neurotics can sexualize almost any area of life, use sex to channel drives which basically have nothing to do with sex, and thereby contaminate the sexual act. Sex can be used in a power struggle as a status symbol: "I'm so sexy, you can't keep up with me." Sex can channel hostility and be a weapon to degrade: "You are so frigid and sick!" "You are impotent and inadequate." A neurotic can give or withhold sex to bribe, blackmail, reward and punish. Sex can be used to degrade oneself: "I despise you, but I can't resist you." The human animal has an enormous capacity for misusing sex in the service of his neurosis, to act out his irrational feelings about himself and others. In our culture the male's self-esteem has always been bound up with sexual prowess. In recent decades sexologists have inflicted this self-consciousness on females too. Women have been grateful for emancipation from the Victorian myth ("Ladies do not enjoy sex,") but the sexologists have given sexual freedom the kiss of death. Authorities who blueprint exactly *how*, *what* and *when* a woman should feel before, during and after each sex act, teach her to observe her reactions with a critical eye, to grade herself pass, excellent, fail. This not only interferes with spontaneity and simple animal pleasure but feeds into her neurotic tendencies, as:

a) shame at failure (see chapter on "The Courage to Fail").

b) anxiety and confusion about her sexual identity: "If I don't feel exactly the way the book says I should, I'm not a real woman."

c) craving for dependency: "It's entirely up to my partner. If only he would read the right books and learn all the proper techniques, then I could enjoy sex the way I'm supposed to."

d) parent-child relationship: "If he really loved me he would read my mind and know exactly what I need without my telling him."

e) projecting her hidden feelings of inadequacy on her partner: blaming, collecting grievances. "I'm O.K.

It's all your fault.''

f) envy: "It isn't fair. All the other women in the world are having this fabulous experience. I'm always being cheated.''

As helpful antidotes to the sexologists I recommend AN ANALYSIS OF THE KINSEY REPORTS by Geddes [33], and an essay, "Some Effects on the Derogatory Attitude Towards Female Sexuality" by Clara Thompson, p. 409, in AN OUT-LINE OF PSYCHOANALYSIS [34].

Why do some couples gradually begin to find sex with one another boring? Kurt Goldstein explains this phenomenon with the "incest taboo." Your earliest love objects were people in your own family and you soon learned that sex with them was forbidden. When you perform the developmental task of adolescence, you outgrow love for family members and are free to fall in love with a stranger. You live with him, learn to know him, and lo and behold, he is no longer a stranger, but a *member of your family*: sexually forbidden. The hidden taboo, this sexual inhibition, feels like boredom, lack of interest in sex with him.

There are several ways out of this bind. For quick, temporary relief, try going off someplace new with him, engaging in a different activity, as if you weren't married. In an unfamiliar setting, involved in nondomestic pursuits, you see one another as strangers once again.

But for longer results you need self therapy. Whenever possible, explore any inappropriate or unpleasant feeling about your partner (see Appendix I, Steps in Self Therapy). Every time you can peel away a layer of apparent emotion and reach a hidden feeling about him, you are a little freer from the unconscious fantasy that he is someone from your original family, a parent or sibling with whom sex is forbidden.

Albert Ellis has a practical approach for people whose inhibitions interfere with pleasure in sex. Their usual method is to avoid thinking about sex, to try to plunge into the act and then find themselves turned off. He advises them to prepare themselves in advance by deliberately recalling old fantasies about sex. Anything that ever happened to you

118

in your life regarding sex, any old experience or daydreams, are part of you. Don't throw them away; use them to get yourself in the mood, says Ellis. If you are lucky, your conscious fantasies can outweigh the unconscious ones which are trying to sabotage pleasure in sex.

3. *Pleasure in activities and the world.* To share interests and experiences with someone you love enhances the pleasure of the activity and strengthens intimacy. When I said earlier that people must pursue their own interests even if they cannot share them with one another, I did *not* mean they can afford to just go their separate ways. It is the shared experiences that cement the relationship and give it meaning.

4. *Self Acceptance.* It is therapeutic to reveal your true self, your weaknesses and fears, to another person and discover that he can still love you, that he is less judgmental of your faults than you yourself are. A relationship of genuine intimacy supplies our need for recognition, acceptance, and confirmation of self.

What happens in a bad marriage? Putney outlines the sad outcome. You depend on your lover's approval to supply the self acceptance you lack. He is projecting all kinds of virtues on you which you really do not posses, and you are afraid to disillusion him, to reveal your true self. This deprives you of *psychological intimacy.*

Unaware of your own inner resources, you project your capacity for fun on him, feel utterly dependent on him for pleasure, and this makes you possessive and jealous, because you are afraid if you lose him you will lose all *pleasure in the world.*

Now, if he begins to discover that you do not measure up to his projections of you, that you are not staying up on that pedestal, he begins to look around for somebody new to project on. You then whip up anger to hide from yourself (and him) how helpless and frightened you are at the possibility of losing pleasure if you lose him. You act out your anger by punishing your partner and depriving yourself of *intimacy* and *sex*.

You begin to shop around for someone else before your first partner has a chance to discover that he is merely projecting on a second person. You discover a new person, you sexualize your projections on him, and "fall in love." Falling in love helps you justify your new projections and your sexualization of them. It also rationalizes your needs for intimacy and sex of which you have been recently deprived.

Putney [11] calls love a neurosis in the sense of Freud's concept of the transference neurosis. Freud discovered that the patient in psychoanalysis tends to experience the analyst as someone from his own past. We know that people in psychotherapy distort the therapists' behavior (see "How to Use a Psychotherapist"). Grotjahn [8] describes how the neurotic treats people in his present family as if they were merely shadows of his original family.

Since Putney sees love as merely a neurosis, he believes it is no basis for marriage. People who enjoy life, he says, can make a good marriage with almost anybody.

Now I agree that a good marriage consists of two people living a full, rich life next to one another, sharing when they can and compromising when they cannot. But I differ with Putney on one important point: *not all nonrational drives are self-defeating*. We cannot afford to depend on the intellect alone for all important decisions. Freud said that while he used his intellect to solve most daily problems, he trusted his unconscious in two areas: in choosing a life work and a life partner.

My own twenty-seven year old marriage is a good one and convinces me that Putney is writing only about bad marriages. I believe in using both *intellect and intuition* in choosing a life partner. If you know the person with whom you are infatuated has values very different from yours, a basic attitude toward life incompatible with your own, you are a fool to marry him—use your head!

On the other hand, it is dangerous to plan a lifetime partnership with someone simply because you both have a great deal in common and you can't find anything very wrong with him. Without that certain spark, that nonrational feeling we call love, life together will be unsatisfying and frustrating

120

THE MEANING OF LOVE

Living day after day in close contact with another person can be a strain. Little things he does, odd quirks and habits will annoy you unless you love him. For some mysterious reason, love can help you tolerate and accept his peculiarities; you may even find them amusing and endearing.

Through the years you are bound to have differences of opinions, arguments, quarrels; you will face serious problems that may shake your marriage. Only love—that nonrational, mysterious extra dimension of a relationship—can supply the essential ingredient: commitment. Without commitment you will feel it's not worth the struggle; you will want to give up.

Then there is the old fashioned virtue of self-sacrifice. (I don't mean martyrdom, the neurotic's weapon for blackmail and manipulation). You may respect, even admire your spouse; feel gratitude toward him for his kindness; hesitate to hurt or exploit him; but only love can make his welfare and happiness seem as important as your own.

When you love someone, his happiness enriches your own, and yet you are not completely dependent on him for your own pleasure. I enjoy serving Bernie a good meal but my relish of the food does not depend on his. Bernie is glad I have finally outgrown my neurotic anxiety about sailing [4], but he can enjoy sailing when I'm not in the mood. Our capacity for pleasure comes from within ourselves.

Abraham Maslow says when you love someone you *value his essential differences* from yourself. He was referring to appreciation of the maleness or femaleness of one's partner. I extend that to include all kinds of differences. Narcissus fell in love with his reflection. Only a narcissistic person wants a mirror image of himself. You would be bored to death living with someone exactly like yourself.

The existential psychologists say that when you love someone *you can see his true potential*: capabilities of which he himself may be unaware. In the early years of our marriage it seemed to me that Bernie saw me as better than I was: good, kind and courageous. His vision of me gave me *goals to strive toward*. I never lied about my weaknesses, never tried to fake these virtues, but often when life presented me with choices I made an effort to be the person he thought I was. For almost three decades I have tried, whenever possible, to *be* good and kind and brave. I have attempted to transcend my tendencies toward selfishness, meanness and cowardice: have experienced the inner conflict between the "good" and "bad" side of me and tried to avoid acting out the side of me that Bernie does not recognize. As described in the chapter, "The Meaning of Self Discipline," I believe this is the path to becoming the person I want to be.

In a *transference relationship* you project on to the other person fantasies of your own forbidden side, your own hidden longings. You distort reality. In *love* you also value attributes of the loved person which you yourself lack, but they are not mere projections. Some of them are active traits in him, others are potentials for such traits which the eye of love perceives. I have described how the lover's perception encourages the loved person to strive toward actualization of these qualities.

These strengths you perceive in him can serve you as a *model for growth*, can help you develop your own hidden strengths. Just as you stretch your psychological muscles to reach the heights of his picture of you, so you can also acquire characteristics you admire in him.

I have always valued certain of Bernie's characteristics which seemed foreign to my nature. I have used him for a model for 27 years and by now I have changed enough to realize that basically we are more like one another than different.

Bernie is unassuming: he has no need to impress anyone. I had always been anxious about my public image, "selling" myself to every Tom, Dick and Harry: everybody's approval mattered to me. The contrast between us helped me recognize that my pattern was neurotic and encouraged me to work on it in self therapy. Today, though still not as relaxed as Bernie, I am no longer constantly on stage, at the mercy of my audience.

Bernie's honesty startled me. All my life I had been lying out of "tact" and general cowardice. I began to feel ashamed of this pattern. Today I still tend to be careful, but with continued gestalt self therapy I am becoming more honest, even though it means rocking the boat, stirring up negative feelings in others.

I am a verbal person. When embarrassed and ill at ease, I talk compulsively. I envied Bernie's quietness. In ackward social situations his silence had a dignity that my eager chatter lacked. Today I am learning how to shut up, to let go, instead of trying too hard to carry the ball.

I am cowardly and a little awed by Bernie's courage. By dint of hard work in self therapy—facing my fear—and experimenting with new behavior I am getting braver. Today I dare to plunge into experiences beyond the wildest dreams of my old timid self.

I have always appeared to be a generous person, but I discovered in self therapy ("The Idealized Self Image" [4]) that my apparent generosity had neurotic overtones. I was basically a grudging giver, my gifts contaminated by hidden motives: the desire for love and gratitude, the wish to feel saintly. From the beginning of our marriage I was struck by the uncomplicated, inconspicuous style of Bernie's generosity, the absence of conflict and ulterior motives.

I began to set a new goal for myself: to give from the heart, ungrudgingly, or not at all. But it is so difficult for a neurotic like me to know my true feelings when I think someone "needs" something from me. Often my first reaction is all giving. Only later do I begin to feel exploited and resentful. With hard work in gestalt self therapy I am beginning to change. Over and over again I have had to experience my inner conflict. One side of me overidentifies with the person who wants something, feels that I *must* give him whatever he wants. The other side, equally irrational, resents being controlled by the needy person. I have not yet completely outgrown this conflict, but I am aware of it and each time I do gestalt self therapy I have a little more freedom to be honest. True, I am losing my old public image of the all-giving saint, but I am becoming a more genuine person and people are finding it easier to trust me.

I have described at length how to use the person you love as a model for your own growth. What about your projections, your own imaginary picture of him? Whenever possible use your projections for self therapy because:

a) These irrational expectations will ruin any relationship. If he attempts to stay on that pedestal, pretends to be the person you want him to be, you are living with a stranger. If he dares to be his true self, you are constantly disappointed in him. When, through your work in self therapy, you can stop trying to fit him into the mold of your own projections, you will begin to know him as he is and the two of you can share true intimacy.

b) Each time you recognize and explore a projection in self therapy you become a little less irrational, you take another step on the path toward health.

In the early years of my marriage, in addition to loving Bernie I also had a full-fledged transference and projected all kinds of fantasies on him. I saw him as the Parent I never had: wise, perfect, one who never made mistakes. The first time he seemed irrational I had an anxiety attack. The Child within me was back in the past with parents who did not know how to protect me. Gradually self therapy taught me that I was an adult, no longer entirely dependent on others. Through the years, as I learned to experience in self therapy the many areas in which I myself am irrational, I found it easier to accept Bernie's right to be irrational once in a while too.

I wanted Bernie to be a strong authority figure and make all the important decisions in our lives. When he asked my advice, expected me to share the responsibility for such decisions, I panicked. The Child within me was screaming, "But I'm only a little girl!" Fortunately, Bernie had no neurotic need to play that Parent-Child game so I turned to self therapy for relief from my fear. True, I was abandoned, left with strangers at an early age, assumed responsibility for myself too soon. As I began to pay attention to the frightened Child within me, stuck back there in the past, the Adult grew stronger. I could put the past in its place, separate it from the present and see myself as my husband's helpmate, not his child.

Another aspect of my projection of Bernie as Parent was my irrational fear of his anger. I was always ashamed of this fear, since he is a kindly, non-violent person, who has no wish to degrade anyone. His occasional flareups of temper are short-lived and invariably followed by remorse. I used self therapy to explore this inappropriate fear. Today it is almost gone.

Side by side with my fantasy of Bernie as Parent was another and very different one: that we were both children, babes in the wood. In order to be safe we had to obey my father. In the first few years of our marriage, when Bernie returned home after the war, my dad had very definite ideas about my husband's career. He proceeded to outline concrete steps he insisted were essential for our future financial security. Bernie listened politely, experimented for a while, and then proceeded along his own lines, under no compulsion to take his father-in-law's advice. When I say "advice" I mean nagging. Dad realized early that his son-in-law was not susceptible to brainwashing, so he concentrated on me. He argued and explained and prophesied a dire future if I failed to make Bernie follow his instructions. Like a frightened Child, I believed him and so *I* nagged my poor husband day and night for weeks, trying desperately to force him to be a Good Child and obey Daddy. Daddy knew best. We were doomed to unknown horrors unless we toed the mark. I suffered chronic anxiety; for the one and only time in my life I broke out all over in hives. Bernie appeared calm and unmoved throughout this siege. Eventually I gave up.

Today I realize he knew what was best for him as Dad, of course, could not. He told me how painful that period was for him, that his surface calm was more apparent than real. He knew I was suffering, he said, but it never occurred to him to give up his autonomy to appease me and my father.

For decades I have been exploring, in self therapy, my fantasies about Bernie. Gradually the fog of projections is clearing away and I can see and appreciate the real person underneath. As transference disappears love flourishes. Marriage becomes more meaningful, a safe, nourishing environment where two people can grow and be themselves.

11. THE OFFICE NEUROSIS

IN HIS book, THE FAMILY NEUROSIS, Grotjahn describes how adults distort their experiences in family life. The intimacy of family living provokes us to react to people in our present families—marriage partners and children—as if they were parents and siblings from our original families. Unresolved problems from the past seep through to contaminate the present.

This same pattern occurs in office life. The intimacy of daily work turns the office staff into a kind of family. Tensions assume exaggerated proportions when they stir up unresolved, hidden problems from the past and we react to them in irrational ways: we feel inappropriate emotions and act out self-defeating behavior.

Many of us unconsciously relate to the boss as to a parent. Years before I ever thought of self therapy I had glimpses of my own irrational attitudes toward people at work. For example, my boss was tough but fatherly--a benevolent despot. Mr. S. knew about my Don Quixote-like scrap for justice in another department before I came to work in his office and he showed a mixture of amusement, admiration, and warmth for my off-beat behavior (very like my own father's attitude toward me in childhood).

One day I heard that Mr. S. had been grossly unfair to another girl in the office. I was horrified—shocked and disappointed. This is an old pattern of mine.

For the first five years of my life I was a loved, only child of affectionate parents. Then I had a horrid surprise: I learned that I could not depend on my parents to protect me, that their own needs took priority over mine. Self therapy has shown me how I compulsively relived this traumatic experience. Time after time I have over-reacted with surprise and disappointment at each discovery that the person in authority is inept or unjust and time after time I have acted out in a self-defeating way [4].

126

THE OFFICE NEUROSIS

Here again the old surprise and disappointment boiled up in me, I rushed in where angels fear to tread. With the naive arrogance of a favorite child, I pranced up to Mr. S. and expressed surprise at what I thought was his uncharacteristic injustice, demanded that he set things right. I was shocked to discover that this time he was not in the least amused or respectful. On the contrary, he was angry and threatened to treat me exactly as he had my unfortunate coworker. From that day on Mr. S. ignored me. Gone was the fatherly smile, the teasing remarks, the spark of recognition. I was cast out, a foster child. I sank into depression. The old, cheery, companionship of my fellow-workers no longer satisfied me. Each morning it became more and more difficult to get up and go to work. Then, after weeks of this misery, a real tragedy struck: my stepmother suddenly died. The shock of her unexpected death, my conflicting feelings about her, love and rage, and the fact that this was the second time I had suddenly lost a mother, pushed me into the intense grief described in the chapter on Loneliness.

We were a close, cozy group in that office and everybody rallied round to comfort me, *including Mr. S.* who was now every bit as kind and affectionate as of old. But now he didn't matter: I didn't care about him. In the face of my loss and real suffering I could look back on the past weeks and laugh at myself. How foolish of me to have wallowed in depression when I had nothing real to complain about! How idotic of me to take Mr. S. and his moods so seriously! How little he mattered in my life, after all. I longed to turn back the clock to those weeks before my stepmother's death.

Many people are irrational about their bosses. There is the man whose work is rewarded with pay raises and promotions, but finds money and status cannot satifsy him. He longs for the special recognition, personal approval, he never got from his father.

A neurotic is someone who failed to get what he needed in the first place, never learned how to get it and still craves it. Mary compulsively relived the same Cinderella role at work she had learned long ago in childhood. She drove herself to perform tasks above and beyond the call of duty, worked overtime without being asked, and tried desperately to earn the love and appreciation from her employer that her mother failed to give her. Her boss had a well-earned reputation as tyrant: demanding, exploitative and unappreciative. When I first knew her, Mary was suffering chronic depression, her weekends spent lying in bed with obsessive thoughts. She acted as if she was trapped: she could not bring herself to change jobs.

Mary had been so severely punished for crying in childhood, that in the early months of self therapy the only way she could channel her painful feelings was to vomit. By the time she learned to cry, she was able to change her job and begin to enjoy weekends. She continued for a long time to live out the old Cinderella pattern: working too hard, hurt and resentful toward her unappreciative employer. But now when things got too painful she could quit her job and try again. After a while she learned to have imaginary encounters with a frustrating boss in gestalt self therapy and turn him into her mother. She learned to dash home and smash cartons during her lunch hour to let off steam. Today Mary is developing latent talents she never knew she had and in general getting more out of life. She is aware of her Cinderella tendency, but no longer compelled to act out in her office. She enjoys her work and is satisfied with her employer's recognition of her value.

Martin's father habitually humiliated and degraded him when he was young. Martin grew up with an "undigested lump" of his father inside him: there is a part of him that needs to act like his father, to degrade others. He frequently projects that tendency on others, especially people in authority. Sooner or later on every job, Martin is hurt and angry because he has distorted something his boss said and feels degraded.

Belle's father was charming and deceptive. All through childhood and youth he tricked her with unfulfilled promises. Today she works for an employer whose apparent warmth masks an exploitative personality and she cannot resist that old combination, though she knows she is unfairly used. Underpaid and over-pressured she drives herself to work too hard. Belle swings back and forth from resentment and shame ("I'm such a sucker!") to an eager desire to use her last ounce of strength helping out in the latest crisis! She is intelligent enough to see what is happening but since she has never used self therapy to work through her conflicted feelings about her father she cannot free herself from this self-defeating pattern: cannot resist a father figure whose seductive warmth is combined with cold exploitation.

I have described elsewhere in this book how the principal of an adult school suddenly dropped my class when I had a good following of eager students. When Mr. B. suddenly pronounced his decision, I was at first surprised and then angry. That anger obsessed me for weeks. One day I was supposed to phone him: when I started to dial, my hand shook so badly I could hardly hold the receiver. I was not aware of any emotion and my first thought was that I must be hungry. But a glance at the clock assured me that I had eaten only a few hours ago, so I realized this must be a symptom of anxiety. That was Step 1, *Recognize an inappropriate feeling.* I put the phone down and went on with Step 2, *Feel the apparent emotion.* It felt like fear. I was afraid of something, but I did not know what. Step 3, *What did I feel before the apparent emotion?* Obsessive anger. Step 4, *What does this remind me of?* I began to think of all my feelings about Mr. B. since I first knew him. I remembered how warm and welcoming he was at our first interview, how he hired me instantly and said, "I can tell by your style that you must be a wonderful teacher." I thought he really liked me. What happened? Why did he want to kick me out now? And what did that remind me of? Suddenly the words rang in my head: "Daddy, I thought you loved me. What happened?" It was my own father's changed attitude that was tormenting me. So affectionate in my childhood! How I looked forward to those weekend visits in foster homes! I turned toward him as toward the sun in those dark years. And then when I grew up he changed; became angry and disapproving. There had been a few years when it seemed I could never please him.

The incident with Mr. B. stirred up those painful years. My anxiety and obsessive anger were covers for old sorrow and loss. I came out of that brief reliving of the past and both the anxiety and intense anger were gone. I could take the whole thing in my stride. Mr. B. was no longer Daddy.

Step 5, *Look for the pattern.* Once in a while, without any conscious awareness of what is going on, I act as if some male authority figure is my father. When he likes me at first and then changes, I cover feelings of rejection with anger and obsessive thinking.

Another aspect of the office neurosis is our tendency to to see our colleagues as siblings. The office staff becomes a family with all the variations of affection, envy and jealousy common among brothers and sisters.

When I was feeling like a daughter to Mr. S, my boss, I felt protective toward the younger girls, guided and helped them exactly as if I were their big sister. I envied and resented the young woman who was office manager. I acted as if she were an older sister assuming too much authority, receiving too many privileges. Then there was Alice. Mr. S. liked and admired Alice: she was his favorite child. He gave her important jobs to do: that meant she was smarter than I. He joked and laughed with her in a special way: that meant she was more loveable. I was eaten up with jealousy, the child within me was crying, "Daddy loves my sister more than me."

Shirley is a young woman who feels left out wherever she works. It seems to her that all the other girls in the office form a close knit clique and that they are deliberately excluding her. Shirley's childhood experiences combined to convince her that she is unlovable, unwanted. She is not aware that her own present behavior appears cold and rejecting. When new people attempt to come near her she pushes them away without realizing what she is doing. She acts unfriendly, suspicious, insincere and gives the general impression that she wants to be left alone. Her expectation of rejection *causes* them to leave her alone.

I have known several people like Shirley. Some of them worked through their hidden feelings about early experiences and were able to change their patterns of behavior. Today they can join the group and feel part of the office family. But those who continue to focus on the faults of others instead of exploring their own hidden conflicts continue, with the same self-defeating behavior, to justify their expectations of rejection in each new work situation. They seem to accept the Cinderella role—and use it to strengthen their blaming attitude toward life. (See "Responsibility and Blame.") They are grievance collectors.

Carl's older brother bullied him in childhood but later in his adolescence and youth attempted to give him the worldly help and guidance his father failed to provide. Carl appreciated this help, but he knew his brother did not really understand him; the early brutality had left its mark. He never felt free to ask for what he needed. Carl is now an adult who relates to an authority figure as to a big brother. He seeks a boss whom he can admire and one who can give him guidance in his work. If the time comes when his boss fails to understand his need, Carl is disappointed in this lack of perception and finds it impossible to ask for what he wants. His tendency is to quit the job and look for another boss who can fulfill his needs.

Here is a hypothetical case to illustrate how self therapy can help you cope with the office neurosis. John is a little boy who bitterly resents his baby brother who displaces him. The younger brother dies and John grows up with the hidden conviction that his anger toward his brother caused that death, that he is a dangerous person, that his anger has magic power. Today he works in an office next to a bully. For some reason, perhaps the age difference between them, this co-worker on a *hidden level*, outside John's conscious awareness, reminds the Child within him of his dead brother. This means it is dangerous to feel anger toward the bully. John hides his anger from himself and acts appeasing. Appeasing behavior always encourages a bully to further bullying, so John's hidden anger boils inside of John. After a while his old defense against anger, appeasing, doesn't work any more—he begins to feel anxiety symptoms. Anxiety looks like fear and a bully always responds to fear with more outrageous behavior, so things get worse. Now suppose John does a little self therapy, peels away one layer and lets himself feel the accumulated rage against his co-worker. The anxiety will disappear. Without going deeper at this time, with no awareness of *why* he has hidden his anger, no insight that the bully represents his dead brother, John will be free to use his intelligence and experience to solve this

131

problem in whichever way best suits his personality. He may simply get up on his hind legs and out-bully his colleague, (a good way to handle a bully), or he may ask for a transfer or quit his job. If he does gestalt self therapy and explores his conflicting feelings, rage and guilt toward his brother, he will be strengthened for future experiences. But even a little bit of self therapy can get him out of an intolerable situation.

12. DEPRESSION

WEBSTER'S DEFINITION: "Depression: a psychoneurotic or psychotic disorder marked by sadness, inactivity and self-depreciation." "A *psychoneurotic or psychotic disorder*": note that depression is not a real emotion like anger, fear, hurt, jealousy, but a *disorder*, a symptom, a mere cover for some genuine emotion; *"sadness"*: when you're depressed you feel sad but you do not know what you are sad about; *"inactivity"*: life loses it savor: nothing is worth doing; *"self-depreciation"*: you are obsessed with thoughts of failure, inadequacy, general worthlessness.

Depression takes over when we turn ourselves off. When you stop feeling, when you screen out real emotion, depression descends like a black cloud, shutting out the vividness and intrinsic value of everything around you. Alienated, isolated from life, only muffled sounds and vague, gloomy outlines can reach you. Depression is a lonely place.

The most important fact to remember about depression is that it is not a real emotion, only a cover for something else. You are depressed because you are acting on the false assumption that some hidden emotion, if you dared to feel it, would be more painful than the depression which disguises it; that you cannot afford to feel that hidden emotion. It is true that sometimes a very forceful, directive person can push you into a hidden feeling too soon, before you are ready to cope with it. But when you are *self*-directed you can experience only those emotions for which you are ready. In self therapy, whenever you peel away the layer of depression and feel the emotion just beneath it, no matter how painful, it lasts only a brief moment and when it goes away, the depression, that long-lingering torment, goes too.

In order to explore the hidden meaning of your depression, you need first to *feel it* and *recognize it as an inappropriate reaction,* the first two steps in self therapy. You must unlearn the destructive lesson taught us all our lives which was: ignore depression, pull yourself together, keep a stiff upper lip. Pay attention to depression. A friend told me she had been suffering depression for weeks. "What did you do with it?" I asked. "Oh, I told myself, Martha pull up your socks!" And so her depression lingered for weeks. She was so busy trying to ignore it that she could not take it seriously enough to discover what lay underneath it.

Some people, especially those who are out of contact with their feelings and chronically depressed, expend a great deal of energy *warding off* depression, trying not to notice it. Rather than face the depression squarely, rather than use it for self therapy, they evolve a variety of techniques for ignoring the spectre that haunts them, pretending it does not exist. Frantically rushing around to see new sights and try new experiences, plunging into dare-devil touches with death are attempts to distract oneself from depression. So is compulsive busyness: busyness on the job or at home, compulsive talking, obsessive thinking, compulsive need to hear music or words continually on radio or television. Those of us who attempt to control our thoughts and feelings in order to ward off depression deliberately try to control people and events around us. Sometimes blinders are put on horses to keep them from seeing trains that might frighten them. We wear blinders to avoid anything that might make us experience our depression and/or the emotion underlying it.

Certain topics of conversation are taboo: "Stop talking about that. You're depressing me." Nobody can depress you. The depression was there long before you heard those words.

Music can be threatening. "I used to find classical music boring but now I love it." Boredom is usually a symptom designed to keep real life at a distance, to avoid letting anything stir up your depression. "Rock-and-roll makes me nervous and jumpy." "Symphony depresses me." Some of us are very vulnerable to music: we have no defense against it; it reaches us on a deeper level than the intellect.

When we are warding off depression, we seek new and "cheerful" sights and try to avoid anything gloomy or frightening.

When I was little I always kept my eyes tight shut in bed

134

because the night was filled with horrible things. Furniture and clothes changed to witches and hobgoblins when the lights went out. Now that I am grown, I can sometimes see pictures when my eyes are closed in that brief period at the edge of sleep, the hypnogogic state. These pictures appear by themselves from some secret place within me and are a source of surprise and entertainment. As soon as a picture appears I can erase it at will. Landscapes, rolling ocean waves and country lanes and meadows in technicolor, are a delight; but faces can be scary. Until recently I used to erase any hint of a face as soon as it arose, for fear it might depress me. My old childhood fear of witches and hobgoblins had become fear of depression.

For years I have made an effort whenever possible to face depression when it comes along and get underneath it to the hidden emotion [4]. I no longer spend days, weeks, months warding off depression. I find that now my approach to hypnogogic pictures has changed. I am able to relax and let myself see whatever pops up out of my unconscious— even faces. I do not have to control each new stimulus for fear of stirring up depression. Now that I am closer to my feelings, depression no longer lurks around every corner. I have not completely discarded my blinders. I still avoid certain novels, movies and plays, but I am more spontaneous, less careful to avoid "dangerous" thoughts.

The chronically depressed person may appear either cool and detached or cheerful and friendly. Either of these two systems can be used to ward off and disguise depression. But whichever system he uses, he tries to avoid people who are in the midst of genuine deep emotion. To witness some-one in the throes of self therapy for example is threatening to him: it may seduce him into feeling the emotion hidden beneath his depression. Because he fears the contagion of pain and does not dare let it rub off on him, he avoids empathy and human closeness when others are suffering. Instead he e x p e r i e n c e s either boredom, embarrassment, detachment, or disapproval. At best, he may feel a super-ficial pity, a pang of discomfort which motivates him to rush in and make the sufferer "feel better" instantly. This "help" serves to shut the other person up, deprives him of the opportunity to stay with his pain long enough to make therapeutic use of it.

The sad thing about warding off depression is that like most defenses it doesn't really work. Freud said, "The trouble with the repressed is it won't stay repressed." Despite all our tricks the depression is always there, just beneath the surface, contaminating all of living.

Another sad result of this kind of avoidance is that when and if you finally get around to doing self therapy the job is much more difficult. A long accumulation of depression is hard to explore. It is much easier to tackle the first appearance of that symptom. In "Detective Work in Self Therapy" [4] I showed how to track down the origin of depression, how to follow the clues to the moment you first noticed it and how to ask yourself questions like, "What happened just before that?" and "What *might* I have been afraid to feel?" Just as in any whodunit mystery story the longer the detective waits before beginning to search for the culprit the colder grow the clues and the fainter the tracks.

13. HOW TO USE A PSYCHOTHERAPIST

RESEARCHERS HAVE studied comparative successes and and failures of different schools of psychotherapy: Freudian, Adlerian, Jungian, Sullivanite, Rogerian, Behaviorist, etc., and discovered that are all about the same. It appears that the therapist's theory about the origin of neurosis is not too significant in terms of his ability to be a helping person. Something else is decisive in getting results. The researchers conclude that the realtionship between therapist and patient is the therapeutic factor.

What to look for in a psychotherapist

The truth is that psychotherapy is an art, not a science; some artists have more talent than others. Also there is such a thing as personality conflict between therapist and patient as between any two people.

After about four sessions with a psychotherapist you should be able to answer *yes* to the following questions: Do I feel safe to express my true feelings? Can I share problems I have not dared to tell others? Will he accept my "bad" feelings and thoughts without punishing or rejecting me? Does he care about me? Does he see me as a real person, not just a case history? Is he trying to understand how I feel, not simply fitting me into a category?

If, at the end of four sessions, your answer to any of these questions is *no*, shop around for another therapist. If the answer is *yes*, and months later you begin to say *no*, that is just part of the negative transference. You will then be ready to explore these feelings as part of the therapeutic experience.

Do not resign yourself to therapy with someone merely because you "believe in" his theories about the origin of neurosis, because he is a Freudian or Jungian or Rogerian. I am always amazed that people who have no hesitation shopping around for a better plumber act helpless about choosing a psychotherapist. Surely your psyche is as precious as your toilet and deserves the best you can get!

One of my students, Myra, told me of her weekly sessions with Dr. X for two years. "He was so clever," she said. "I admired his intelligence. But he always looked at me coldly as if I were something under a microscope." Tears came to her eyes. "I felt he never really gave a damn about me!" I wanted to know how she could waste two years of her life that way. Why didn't she try another therapist? At first she could not explain, but she went away and mulled it over and later came back to tell me, "By the time you're ready to go into therapy you've had so many failures in your life, you feel like a nothing. Your self-esteem is all the way down. So when you finally get around to asking for help and this big authority person looks at you as if you were a bug, something small and inferior, you're ready to accept yourself at his evaluation. It doesn't occur to you to question his attitude." Later she dared to try again and finally found the right therapist for herself.

I am always sad when I meet a person who has lost all faith in professional psychotherapy after one bad experience. Because he has failed to look around and experiment, because he hung on too long with a therapist who did not suit him from the start, he now condemns the whole profession and deprives himself of necessary help. He would surely not swear off the medical profession just because one physician disappointed him.

What is psychotherapy?

Various psychotherapists, whose clients have been my students, tell me they consider my self therapy techniques good preparation for and an adjunct to professional therapy. But I see it the other way around. I view professional therapy (which by its nature is temporary) as a preparation for and an adjunct to self therapy—a life-long discipline. A good listener (the therapist) gives you permission to take yourself seriously. His concern and respect help you tolerate the shame and guilt which go with self therapy. Once you have learned how to make use of a professional listener you will know how to find friends who can listen on occasion when you need to think out loud.

It is naive and self-defeating to look for a Magic Helper, to expect the therapist to ''do'' something to you which will ''cure'' you. Freud said he hoped psychoanalysis would never become a monopoly of the medical profession. The medical model for psychotherapy is very misleading. Only you yourself can assume responsibility for your own emotional growth. You must do the work yourself; no-one can do it for you.

What is the work of psychotherapy?

1. To learn to recognize inappropriate reactions.
2. To feel your apparent emotions even when you are labeling them irrational (neurotic defenses).
3. To explore the apparent emotions and experience the hidden feelings underneath.
4. To experience your inner conflicts.
5. To experiment with new behavior.

Any psychology student can teach you how to theorize about your case history, how to make educated guesses about your unconscious motivation. This kind of intellectual activity is not, itself, therapeutic.

The helping person, the good therapist, is one who can provide a therapeutic atmosphere where you can dare to take the plunge from the known to the unknown, from the apparent feeling (conscious) to the hidden one (unconscious).

Why is this plunge so difficult? Why do we avoid our hidden emotions? The frightened Child within, still stuck in the unresolved problems of the past, is caught up in the old, forbidden emotions: rage, envy, jealousy, etc. The Parent lies in waiting, ready to pounce on these old, forbidden feelings as soon as they come to light, to punish the Child with shame, guilt, fear, self hatred, helplessness, etc. No wonder we learn to keep the Child out of sight, to avoid rocking the boat. But that is a poor bargain we try to make with the Parent. You cannot appease a tyrant. The Parent in your head is punishing you all the time anyway with depression, anxiety, tension, psychosomatic illness for your hidden feelings, and because they are hidden you don't know what you are being punished for. You live with this punishment for unknown sins but ignorance is no excuse before the law. Your conscious ignorance of the Child's activity does not pacify the judging Parent. On the contrary, the less awareness the Adult has, the more trouble the Child stirs up.

How can the Adult help protect the Child
from the cruel Parent?

Suppose you dare to let the Child feel rage toward your mother: your gentle, feeble old mother was once a frustrating power; the Child is still back there in the past and knows nothing about the present. You experience the rage and then the Parent inflicts a pang of guilt for that forbidden emotion. After a moment of guilt, the Adult says, "My bad thoughts have no magic power. I'm not hurting my mother. My anger isn't doing her any harm." The rational, practical Adult is protecting the irrational Child against the irrational Parent. You have dared to feel both *the rage and the guilt* and then both are gone. The Parent has no power to torture the Child with long term depression, etc., as long as the Adult is functioning. The whole experience is therapeutic: the Child is more comfortable having vomited up some of that old junk, the Adult has had a chance to flex its muscles and is strengthened, the Parent backs down and is a little weaker.

What happens when the Adult is too weak to protect
the Child against the Parent?

The Child, sometimes frightened and appeasing, sometimes rebellious and daring, fights a never-ending battle with the Parent. This battle goes on in secret. You hardly ever know your true feelings: they are covered up with psuedo emotions (fake anger covering fear, fake fear covering anger, etc.) depression, anxiety, tension, psychosomatic illness.

Furthermore, the less responsibility the Adult takes in your life, the less aware you are of the Child's suffering, the more active the Child becomes. If you don't hear him whimper, he screams; if you ignore his screams he has to act. This means the Child not only feels forbidden emotions which bring forth punishment from the Parent, but he actually forces you to behave in self-defeating ways. This is what psychologists call "neurotic acting-out". Now the Child has two judges. The Parent who is more outraged than ever and the Adult who is horrified at actions contrary to his values. The punishment (depression, anxiety, etc.) grows more intense, the Child becomes more frustrated and acts out more and receives more punishment and you are stuck in a horrible vicious circle.

It would be wonderful if the therapist could enter into the battle, cross swords with the Parent, and be the Child's champion. When you tell him, "My mother frustrated me when I was little, but I realize now she couldn't help it. She was doing the best she could. I'll feel so guilty if I get mad at her now," your therapist may reassure you, "You have a perfect right to be angry, and since you are not planning to punish her now, you don't have to feel guilty."

It sounds as if he is telling the Child within you, "Don't worry. Go ahead and feel angry. I'll protect you from the cruel Parent," and to the Parent, "Don't you dare punish this Child. I'm here to protect him." Unfortunately, neither Child nor Parent can hear your therapist. They are functioning back there in the past and are not able to understand present-day logical reasoning. The only part of you that can hear the therapist is the *Adult.*

The therapist *cannot intervene in the inner battle between Child and Parent.* Only the Adult in you can assume such responsibility for yourself.

What is the psychotherapist's role in this battle?

The therapist can talk to the Adult. He can point out reality, bring the Adult thinking processes up to modern standards, free it from the obsolete anachronistic reasoning of the Child and the Parent.

The therapist also serves as a model for the Adult: a) He demonstrates how a rational person uncontaminated by your particular history sees your problem. He opens the door to the fresh air of common sense when you are befogged with irrational conflicts. b) In his relationship with you, he teaches you by example how to be more accepting of the Child within you, how to set limits to the cruel Parent. The therapist strengthens the Adult, prepares it for the task of therapy.

What is the Adult's role in therapy?

Communication between the Adult (conscious) and the Child and Parent (unconscious) is strictly one-way. In the midst of a therapeutic experience the Adult can hear what the Child and Parent are saying. If, after such an experience you "resolve" to stop feeling that way because it is irrational, you are kidding yourself. The Adult cannot tell the Child or Parent how to feel. They are functioning in an earlier stage of your development and they *cannot hear you* any more than they can hear your therapist.

You may think, after your therapist talks sense to you, that the Adult can promise the Child, "Go ahead. Feel furious toward Mother. I'll protect you from the punishing Parent. You don't have to feel guilt." The Child cannot hear and the *promise is false.* You cannot stop the Parent from punishing with guilt.

What role does the Adult play in your inner struggle?

Like a good group leader, the Adult is a participant observer who can stop the action before it goes too far. This is my approach as leader in my communication workshops: two people confront one another in a painful encounter, tackle a problem they cannot resolve since both are irrational at the same time. I do not stop the action until each has expressed his feelings fully and intensely. After a while, if they reach an impasse and tend to repeat themselves, punishing one another indefinitely, unproductively, hanging on to their apparent emotions and whipping them up to avoid any true self-awareness, I intervene. I step in and sum up what has happened, accept each person's right to his feelings and show that I can see both sides even though they are deaf to one another. I stop the endless, boring punishment and self-justification and give them a glimpse of reality—the fact that they are being irrational.

HOW TO USE A PSYCHOTHERAPIST

In therapy, the Adult plays the same leadership role. The Child in you dares to feel rage toward your mother for something she did years ago. Then the Parent pops up with guilt. *Let yourself feel the guilt* for a few minutes. Don't try to avoid it just because your therapist told you guilt is irrational. Of course it is irrational. Everything you feel in self therapy is irrational, it belongs to your earlier self; but you cannot afford to skip over it. This is an essential part of the work of therapy—feeling the irrational junk. Like a good group leader the Adult lets Child and Parent express their feelings, rage (Child) and guilt (Parent), for a brief while. Then the Adult steps in and stops the punishment from continuing on and on. The Adult, strengthened by your therapist, can speak up in a rational way; to the punishing Parent, "Nonsense! I'm not hurting my mother. My thoughts have no magic power. I'm just spitting up old stuff from the past"; to the angry Child, "I'm not small and helpless any more. I can live without Mother's understanding."

Timing is the impotant factor in this process. If the leader (Adult) intervenes too soon, the combatants (Child and Parent) do not have time to air their grievances. The strong feelings (rage or guilt) get pushed underground where they keep thrashing around until they burst out at an unexpected moment and cause trouble (neurotic acting-out, neurotic symptoms). If the Adult waits too long to function on a reasoning level, the rage and/or guilt go on and on and can turn into depression, anxiety, etc.

Suppose the Adult is contaminated by the Child or the Parent. It is then too irrational, too weak to be of any use in that inner battle. When the Adult joins the Parent in scolding the Child, ("How dare you be angry at your Mother. You know how hard she tried to do right. How can you be so unjust?") not accepting the Child's right to be irrational, two things are likely to happen. 1) Instead of feeling refreshed and strengthened by your therapeutic experience you may suffer depression, anxiety or other neurotic symptoms. 2) It will be harder to do self therapy next time: the Child feels unsafe with a weak Adult, and hesitates to speak out.

If the Adult is contaminated by the Child, it pretends that the present is just like the past. Instead of briefly feeling the rage that was once appropriate, and coming out of it with a clear, comfortable mind, you will stay with the rage, as if you were still a small child at your mother's mercy. You will then either 1) act out, in self-defeating behavior, that inappropriate rage toward your mother or others whom you imagine are trying to do what your mother once did, or 2) not daring to channel the rage, will keep it hidden and feel weak and helpless or suffer anxiety, depression, etc.

In these two cases, the Adult takes sides, fails to act as a responsible leader when Child and Parent confront one another.

Each time the Adult acts like a strong leader it gives the Child courage to speak out next time. The Child learns from experience that it is safe to openly experience a "dangerous" emotion. It realizes that although the Adult cannot prevent the Parent from punishing with some guilt, etc. it will stop the punishment before it gets too bad. The Child also learns that it will not be stuck indefinitely with a painful feeling, rage, etc.; will not be encouraged to act out in self defeating ways: the Adult will see reality and assume responsibility for rational feelings and actions.

There is no short cut to growth. When your therapist says, "You *don't have to feel* shame, or guilt or fear about that; it's irrational," do not take him literally. He is really talking to the Adult in you, teaching you that it is irrational to accept the verdict of the Parent. Your job is to experience the battle between Parent and Child *first*; then let the Adult come to the rescue. Do not kid yourself into thinking you can bypass that battle.

Nobody ever got better in the therapist's office

Some people think all they have to do is get closer to their unconscious and they will automatically, magically become healthy. But all the insights and therapeutic experiences in the world will not change you unless you apply your new self knowledge to real life. When you develop self awareness, knowledge of your self-defeating patterns, when you experience the hidden feelings that cause those patterns, you are ready for another, equally important responsibility. You must begin to experiment with new behavior. Bruno

HOW TO USE A PSYCHOTHERAPIST

Bettleheim [21] explained that we are largely what we appear to be, that our actions, not our thoughts, make us. Ideas are not enough; hell is paved with good intentions. Genuine change comes from the combination of true self-knowledge plus *new behavior*. Psychotherapy does not take place in a vacuum: you cannot merely contemplate your navel for years and suddenly burst out into the world, a healthy person. Psychotherapy is slow, hard work; translating irrational actions into hidden emotions and then transmitting new, rational awareness into rational behavior. We are what we are becoming. Today's action helps make me the kind of person I will be in the future.

Communication

People sometimes ask, "Why do I need a professional psychotherapist? I have a good friend to confide in. What can a therapist do that my friend cannot do?" The therapist can give you a brand new experience in human relations.

Most of us are so busy "handling" people, warding off disapproval, rejection, punishment, that we never dare speak the complete truth to another person about our feelings toward him. We are often too proud (ashamed) to show hurt, fear, envy, jealousy; too fearful to express rage; too shy to proclaim love. The professional therapist is by temperament and training prepared to accept all your feelings about him. He expects them; they are part of the therapeutic experience.

The fortunate child is one who can stamp his little foot and yell, "You're a mean Mommy and I hate you!" secure in the knowledge that Mommy will continue to love him. Few of us have been so lucky. Most of us have learned to avoid speaking the truth about our feelings toward others, especially people who matter most to us. Without this kind of communication, genuine intimacy is impossible; human relationships degenerate to games people play [5].

If you dare to use the professional therapeutic relationship as an experiment in real communication, you give yourself a second chance to experience what you missed in childhood with an accepting parent. You learn a new and healthier way of being close to people.

145

Honest communication with your therapist can be therapeutic in unexpected ways. Betty complained to me about her psychiatrist: "I've had a few sessions with her and I'm going to quit. There's not a drop of human warmth in her. She's just a cold fish. I could never open up to such a person."

"Will you tell her why you're quitting?"

Betty was horrified. "Of course not."

"Why not?"

"Oh, I couldn't say such a cruel thing to anyone."

"What do you think would happen to her?"

"She'd be so terribly hurt, it would crush her. How could she stand it?"

"How do you usually handle people like this in real life?"

"I get away from them as fast as possible. I just avoid them."

But she admitted that these days, out in the working world, and no longer at home with small children, it was getting harder and harder to run away from people. We talked about an old pattern: her compulsive need to protect everybody from any pain or discomfort. I reminded her that her mother was a weak, fragile person to whom Betty never dared speak the truth for fear of devastating her; of the load of rage and frustration piled up from those careful years.

"Try something different this time," I advised. Level with this woman, this parent figure, whom you imagine is so fragile. See what happens. I'm not saying stay with her, just speak out before you run away."

So Betty dared to speak the truth and discovered to her amazement that the psychiatrist was not weak like her mother, but, on the contrary, appeared strong and tough. She took that criticism in her stride, apparently unmoved and, in Betty's opinion, cooler than ever.

This final conference was therapeutic for Betty. She was able to experience her overprotectiveness and her resentment toward her mother. In relating to "cold" women at work she found she could be more rational now.

HOW TO USE A PSYCHOTHERAPIST

Transference

From time to time in daily life you meet a person with whom you relate as if he were someone from your past, someone with whom you have unfinished business, unresolved problems. You tend to distort his words and actions and react inappropriately to them. You "read" his mind (incorrectly), "guess" his motives (incorrectly) because of your own hidden feelings. The Child within you confuses the present with the past, today's people with yesteryear's.

The very nature of the therapeutic relationship, your dependency on this helping person, makes transference almost inevitable. You can expect to over-react to many of his words, facial expressions, bodily movements. Be prepared to feel intense emotions about him—hate, love, fear, jealousy—which the Adult in you suspects are inappropriate, irrational.

If you are neurotic that means you failed to get what you needed in the first place, are still trying to get it and never learned how. Whatever you were deprived of—your mother's love, your father's respect, your sister's friendship—the Child within still seeks desperately in self-defeating ways.

When you meet someone who seems (to the Child) to fit the pattern of the depriving person from your past, you try to control his attitude toward you with your own special system: manipulating, bullying, appeasing, impressing, flattering, blackmail ("I'll kill myself if you reject me!"), etc. You gravitate toward the person who has a neurotic tendency to play your game, whose problems dove-tail with yours. If you like to bully people you will find someone who needs to be bullied. If you like to whine about your misfortunes, you can find someone who loves to offer sympathy. If you enjoy being told what to do, you will discover a friend who wants to plan your life for you.

Whatever games you typically play with others in your life, you will inevitably try to play with your therapist. If he has not been damaged in that particular area, he will not be tempted to play your game. Unfortunately, Maslow tells us only one in 1000 people are completely healthy. That means you may just hit your therapist in a vulnerable area, in which case you can seduce him into playing and slow up your therapy considerably. Fritz said most people go into therapy, not to get better, but to play games with the therapist. He believed the therapist's duty is to deliberately frustrate the patient's attempt to play games. This puts a tremendous burden on the therapist and assumes that he is either a) healthy in all the areas where his patients are sick, or b) continually practicing self therapy in order to avoid falling into pitfalls when his patients' problems coincide with his.

I am teaching people *to assume responsibility* for their own growth. *You* must keep constantly in mind what your self-defeating patterns are, what kinds of games you tend to play, how you usually distort. Whenever you notice yourself: a) over-reacting to your therapist's behavior and/or b) trying to force him to change, use that material for therapy.

Some of the special ways you can frustrate the therapist, sabotage the therapeutic process are: 1) demand that he answer endless questions, intellectualize about your case history as if you were merely an interested professional bystander; 2) refuse to listen to any interpretations at all; 3) pretend to accept his interpretations when they seem incorrect to you; 4) fantasy that he can read your mind and understand you perfectly with little or no communication; 5) blame him because he cannot understand you.

If you are aware of your self-defeating patterns with people, if you recognize the kind of games you play, watch for your tendency to use them with your therapist. Be prepared to experience him as someone from your unresolved past—your over-protective but unloving mother, your disapproving father, your jealous sister, your envied brother, etc. As soon as you have any clue that your feeling is irrational, *use it* for self therapy. This is the quickest way to grow. The more autonomous you are, the more responsibility you take for your own therapy, the sooner you will get healthy. This is what psychotherapy is all about and the harder you work at it, instead of waiting for the Magic Helper, the greater your progress.

In a paragraph above, *Communication*, I described the benefits of speaking the truth about your feelings toward your therapist. However, communication is no substitute for therapy. Yes, by all means tell your therapist whenever you are hurt or scared or angry. Any time you suspect he is angry or rejecting or disapproving, ask him, check it out. But, when you suspect your feeling is irrational, part of the transference relationship, do not stop at mere communication. Go on from there to self therapy; look for the hidden feeling.

Some patients exploit the therapeutic relationship. The therapist becomes a scapegoat for all the years of frustration. They act out all their irrational feelings, use him for a punching bag: "You are a rotten therapist. You're stupid, bad, etc." This punishment represents the patient's resistance against therapy. Of course it would be wonderful if the therapist could get in there and do battle with your resistance, fight with the voice in your head that is trying to stop you from growing, that is hanging on to your neurosis. Unfortunately, as explained earlier in this chapter, the therapist cannot communicate directly with that hidden part of you. The best he can do is reason with the Adult in you. It is your responsibility to experience the inner struggle between the striving for health and the resistance.

If you keep indulging yourself by merely acting out, neglecting to follow up irrational feelings with self therapy, you defeat yourself in two ways.

I. Each time you act out an inappropriate reaction, an irrational emotion, and then waste it, you are throwing away a precious opportunity for self therapy. You are slowing up your own growth.

Dan is a good example. He frittered away most of his therapeutic hour in superficial talk and waited for the last five minutes to get to his real problems and feelings. When he begged for an extension of time Dr. Y at first gave in to this demand. But when the pattern continued in other sessions, the therapist began to set firm limits. He insisted that Dan leave at the end of the alloted time in fairness to the other patients. Dan felt angry and deprived. Although the Adult in him was faintly aware that he was making an unreasonable demand and that this pattern might have a hidden meaning, he deliberately hung on to his apparent feelings, whipped himself up to righteous indignation and acted out:

blamed, scolded, punished. Dan threw away an opportunity to do the real work of therapy, to explore his irrational feelings toward Dr. Y and the therapeutic hour. By turning this incident into a power struggle between himself and Dr. Y, he avoided looking within, the true work of therapy.

Years ago in my first gestalt workshop under Fritz Perls I formed an instant transference, "fell in love" at first sight, but Fritz rejected me. At mealtime he literally turned his back on my eager conversational gambits, during breaks he snubbed me unmercifully. Though he was supportive and helpful whenever I did the real work of gestalt therapy during sessions, I suffered such obsessive jealousy and deprivation that for days I could not eat or sleep properly, just dragged myself around with a blinding headache, and cried day and night. I used every trick I knew to win Fritz's approval and affection but nothing worked. He told me he was repelled by a certain "cute little girl" voice I used, an old defense that functioned whenever I felt most insecure.

Unlike Dan, above, I used this opportunity. In desperation, simply to stay sane, I had to use self therapy hour after hour, whenever I was alone during the day and far into the night when I could not sleep. At long last, late one night, after days of hard, hard work, I arrived at this insight, "I have avoided growing up. I tried to remain Daddy's little girl in order to hold his love and IT NEVER WORKED! He stopped loving me anyway. To hell with him! I give up."

I had been floundering around in that impasse for days—how to *make* Fritz (my father) love me. Suddenly I was free. I found a new way: I simply did not care any more. I accepted my helplessness and felt resigned. Exhausted, I slipped into my first good night's sleep. Next morning, the mood of fatigue and resignation combined with a kind of relaxed contentment. My headache was gone; breakfast tasted delicious; I stopped crying. To my surprise Fritz and the group were delighted with my *new voice*. The anxious little-girl tone was gone and I sounded like a relaxed grown-up woman.

After that experience my attitude toward my work began to change. For the first time I saw myself as an adult doing the real work of the world, not just a gifted child playing. I was a professional! I began to lead self therapy workshops and I wrote a book.

What is transference all about ?

Someone frustrated you long ago and today you discover a new person who *seems* to be frustrating you in the same way. You distort his words and actions to fit your preconceived expectations. (Sometimes you act in a provocative manner to make him frustrate you; you set yourself up for this treatment, the self-fulfilling prophecy.) Often, when you think someone is doing to you exactly what was done to you in the past, you begin to treat him that way without realizing it. *You do to him what you accuse him of doing to you.* You are haunted by the person in your past who frustrated you: a) you "see" him in others, where he does not exist; b) he acts *through you* as through a medium. Whatever you hate most in others is something you yourself do, or would like to do, to others.

Many of my self therapy students develop transferences on me. Typically, whenever a student distorts my behavior, (imagines I am doing what his mother or father or sibling used to do to him) he promptly begins to treat me exactly the way that person from the past treated him. If he thinks I am putting him down, not respecting his intelligence, he shows me how stupid I am. If he suspects I am trying to brainwash him with my ideas, he begins to force his theories down my throat.

One of the best ways to use your therapist is to use your negative feelings and suspicions about him for self therapy. Keep in mind that the traits in others of which we are most intolerant are often traits we ourselves possess, lumps of undigested people from the past which nauseate us in others. We have not yet digested them (integrated into our personalities) nor vomited them up.

Years ago, when I was in private therapy, I drove to my session one day obsessed with material left over from the previous meeting. It seemed to me my therapist had failed to fulfill a certain promise he made me and I was bitterly disappointed. As soon as I came in I burst out, "I'm so mad at you! You promised . . . etc., etc." and as soon as I had whipped up enough rage to use it for self therapy I asked myself, "What does this remind me of?" and the answer was, "Just like my father!" I went back to my childhood, to my father's broken promises and let those old disappointments come alive. I *used* the present anger toward my therapist to open the door to the past, to experience the deep hurt I had avoided all those years.

When I was finished, my therapist explained the present problem from his point of view, but it did not matter any more. I had been over-reacting because of the old, unfinished business with my father, and now I was comfortable. The immediate situation was no longer a problem.

Years later in gestalt self therapy I was able to go deeper into my feelings of disappointment exploring my hidden attitudes toward my mother. She, who was so warm and affectionate the first five years of my life, suddenly deserted me; she failed to fulfill the promise of love. Later exploring my relationship with my self therapy students, I recognized how I disappoint them in the same way, how the warmth and concern I feel for them often appears to be a promise I cannot fulfill. The Child within the student is looking for the Perfect Parent who will take care of him, undo the tragic past, and to the person in a transference I appear to fill that role. The kind of love I feel for him is misleading: I can never supply the "needs" of that starved Child; I fail to fulfill my "promise". In gestalt self therapy I am still experiencing the struggle between two sides of myself: the wish to be the mother I never had and the fear that I am just like my mother.

To sum up: each time you act out an irrational feeling toward your therapist without using it for self therapy you waste a precious opportunity to grow; each time you use that irrational feeling to explore what lies beneath, you are doing the real work of therapy.

II. Another danger in too much acting out: You jeopardize your relationship with your therapist just as you do with others in your life.

The best trained therapist, with all the good will in the world, is after all, only human. He can comfortably accept your irrational negative feelings *when you are using them for therapy*. The pleasure in the creative process of psychotherapy and his concern for you gives him strength to take a lot of junk you have to dish out.

But if you are continually living out the role of the kicking, screaming baby, treating him like a *thing* instead of a fellow human, expecting him to love you while you dump all kinds of garbage on him just for the pleasure of releasing decades of rage you never channeled before, you are headed for trouble. If *you are not doing the real work of therapy*, but simply indulging your lifelong desire to let off steam, your therapist may not be able to take it indefinitely. Without the creative satisfaction of watching you grow, the strain of chronic punishment over too long a period of time may cool him off.

Some people think they can pay for anything. Their fantasy is, "The therapist is just doing this for money. He should be willing and able to take anything I dish out." This projection of the therapist-as-prostitute is worth exploring in gestalt self therapy. The patient should ask himself, "When have *I* sold myself, degraded myself in order to get something—money, status, love, approval?"

No one would chose to listen to people's problems all day long just for money. Therapy is hard work. A therapist is a person who gravitated to this work because of his deep craving to understand people, his curiosity about them and his desire to help. A gifted therapist has, besides these traits, a capacity for love and respect for others regardless of their neurotic patterns. Love cannot be bought. It can be weakened or even killed by too much brutality.

This is *not* a warning to "handle" your therapist, to appease or manipulate or play whatever game you play with others in your life. Be as open and genuine as possible, more authentic than you ever dared before. Communicate; don't act out. *Say*, "I feel angry, hating." And try to use your irrational feelings for self therapy whenever possible, rather than limiting yourself to the pleasures of hitting a hired punching bag.

GESTALT SELF THERAPY

Wasting the therapeutic hour

Some patients tell me, "All I can do is intellectualize during my session. I can't feel anything." Or worse yet, "My mind goes blank. I don't know what to talk about." The block against feeling and/or thinking is the form your resistance takes. One part of you hates to waste that expensive hour but the other sabotages every attempt to grow.

Techniques for fighting resistance

I. *Before the therapeutic hour*

A. *Preparation.* When I was in private therapy I used to review the week's events while driving to the therapist's office: "Have I swept anything under the rug? What painful emotions did I ward off? How do I feel today? Any hint of depression, anxiety, tension?" By the time I began the therapeutic hour I was ready to plunge into self therapy.

B. *Unfinished business.* Tell him about feelings you avoided discussing last time or those which cropped up later. Were you hurt when he laughed? Frightened because you thought he looked disapproving? Angry when he interrupted you? Disappointed when he misunderstood you? Your feelings about your therapist are a most important part of therapy and he cannot read your mind. It is up to you to keep the lines of communication open. Hopefully, when you start talking about emotions you felt last week, you will be able to experience them again and use them for therapy: What does this remind you of? Who did this to whom long ago?

II. *After the therapeutic hour*

Some patients are only able to intellectualize during the hour, talk about their case histories in an emotionless, impersonal way. This kind of discussion is good preparation, but not a substitute for therapy. Often that hour of talk may stir up emotions you are able to experience later. In this case you must consider the period *after* you leave your ther-

154

apist's office part of the therapeutic experience. Plan to sit in a quiet place for a while and continue the work of therapy.

Some of my students carry paper and pencil and do their most creative therapy work in their cars after sessions. They get their feelings down in black and white and this helps to experience them more intensely and explore them in self therapy.

III. *The here-and-now*

A. The body has its own language; pay attention to it. Describe all signs of tension: clenched teeth, tight thigh muscles, pounding heart, uneven breath. Sometimes, just talking about these physical symptoms can let you experience the emotion. I have heard people say, ''I'm not feeling anything.'' and then suddenly burst into tears while describing their bodily signs of anxiety, depression, anger, etc.

B. Have a gestalt self therapy encounter with your therapist. Explore your fantasies about him:

Therapist: Now don't get emotional. Just tell me your problem and let's solve it intelligently. Don't start crying and carrying on. See how calm and reasonable I am. Be like me.

or—

Therapist: Go ahead, make a damn fool of yourself. Let yourself go. I'll sit here and gloat over your lack of control. It will make me feel so superior.

or—

Therapist: God, you disgust me, you poor sick thing. *I* have no problems. I'm so strong and you're so disgustingly weak.

C. Have a gestalt self therapy encounter with your resistance, a dialogue between the two sides of yourself—one wants to feel and be genuine and the other tries to stop it:

155

> Resistance: Don't you dare make a fool of yourself I'll make you feel so ashamed you won't be able to raise your head. Don't be weak. That's disgusting.

> or—

> Resistance: You have no right to feelings. I'll keep you in prison, cold and lonely and turned off because you don't deserve to feel alive. I'll keep you dead.

Actually, if you keep working on III B above, (the encounter with your therapist) you will eventually get to III C, (encounter with your resistance) since you are projecting your own resistance on him. It *seems* to you that he is not giving you freedom to feel. The truth is *you* are not giving yourself that freedom. It is true that some therapists are more gifted than others in helping patients feel comfortable and safe with their emotions. But, in the final analysis, it is your own fantasy that you need someone's permission to feel. I have known people who stay frozen and resistant with the most accepting, warm, permissive therapists, and others who can go right into their feelings in the presence of apparently cool, unresponsive therapists.

Remember that professional psychotherapy is an aid to self therapy, not a substitute for it. There are no Magic Helpers. We ourselves must do the work of therapy, assume responsibility for our own growth.

14. LONELINESS

FOR YEARS my students requested a lecture on loneliness, but I kept avoiding it. It seemed to me that loneliness was something foreign to me and I pride myself on always teaching from first-hand experience, not on material merely gleaned from books. However, at last I gave in to popular demand and began to collect available literature on the subject.

One day, when I thought I had accumulated enough material I sat down to plan the lecture and found myself blocking. I just couldn't seem to get on with it. I kept compulsively tracking down references, reading and rereading relevant passages in my collection. Then I began to recognize this was an inappropriate reaction; Step 1 in self therapy (appendix I). Step 2, *Feel the apparent emotion.* Mild anxiety, afraid I had insufficient material to make up a lecture. (This is an old, recurrent symptom which I knew was irrational since I always have too much material, can never stay within the two-hour lecture schedule). Step 3, *What other feeling did I have just before the apparent emotion?* Lack of involvement, detachment from the whole subject of loneliness, the conviction that I was not qualified to lecture on loneliness because I did not know how it felt. Step 4, *What does this remind me of?* I could not remember anything relevant. I tried asking myself, *What do I seem to be doing?* I seemed to be running away from the subject of loneliness. What memory could I possibly be running from? And then I suddenly remembered the lonely foster child I once was: those homeless years living on the fringes of other people's families. For a brief moment I could feel a pang of that old loneliness. Then I understood. Step 5, *Look for the pattern.* I had been trying all my adult life to forget about that lonely child, to stay in my fortunate present and pretend the past never happened. It was that effort to forget which blocked my thinking about loneliness.

GESTALT SELF THERAPY

There are two kinds of loneliness: *real loneliness*, a creative experience, and the *neurotic fear of loneliness*. [14]. A local newspaper once interviewed housewives who had recently settled in a California suburb. They described the isolation and loneliness of new arrivals in the community. Several women who read the article sneered at those lonely people. "With good public libraries and all these concerts and plays," they told each other, "any intelligent woman can live a satisfying life here. Why don't they join the PTA or the League of Women Voters?" I happened to know that each of these judgmental women, when they first moved to that community were themselves depressed at their isolation, far from old friends and familiar activities.

They had never gone beyond the neurotic fear of loneliness. They had not allowed themselves to actually face the loneliness, experience it deeply, and so all they could do now was try to forget it ever happened. When you are covering up a painful experience you have little empathy for others in the same boat. You are intolerant of them.

The neurotic fear of loneliness is basically a fear of failure. In our present culture it is considered shameful to be lonely. The mass media emphasizes the importance of winning friends and influencing people; popularity is equated with success [15]. Until recently adolescence was accepted as a period of loneliness. Popular novels used to portray the painful loneliness of youth's search for identity [16], [17]. But today young people have money to spend so the mass media, directed toward them, teach them that adolescence is the happiest time of their lives, that they are supposed to belong to a crowd of other fun-loving, carefree youngsters and never be lonely. If they *are* lonely, the message implies, there is something very wrong with them. The Madison Avenue myth feeds into the American's neurotic fear of loneliness.

I have often felt the neurotic fear of loneliness. I remember periods in my girlhood when I had to go to the movies alone. When I came out of the theatre I tried to slink invisibly through the streets, convinced that the casual passerby was looking at me in scornful pity—a girl who had to go to the movies alone! Sometimes I would mask my shame with a mysterious, dreamy smile designed to prove how self-sufficient I was, lost in fascinating thoughts, a person who chose solitude on this particular occasion, despite innumerable people clamoring for her company.

Then there was the New Year's Eve when I was twenty. I had just broken with my steady boy friend and was dateless. I don't know about young people today, but in my time it was a shameful sign of failure to be without a New Year's Eve date and I planned to hide my disgrace at home. My best friend and her date insisted I spend the evening with them, and against my better judgment I allowed myself to be persuaded. Those were depression days and we spent a frugal evening at a foreign film in Manhattan followed by a late supper in Chinatown. On the way home in the subway train, I prayed we would not bump into anyone I knew. To my horror, a girl I knew dashed over to sit with us. To cover my embarrassment at being caught dateless on New Year's Eve, I lied. I carefully explained that my date had to work that night and we had just dropped him off. I was so obsessed with my shame that it wasn't until years later I realized she was all *alone*.

In those days I used to go to concerts with my girl friend and it always seemed as if all the world were paired off except us and that other people pitied us.

Years later with a husband of my own at home, I was embarrassed to attend a concert without a woman friend: people might notice my isolation and pity me for being friendless. I used to bring a book to read during intermission, concentrating hard to appear self-reliant and independent—a woman who *wanted* to be alone. After years of self therapy, without deliberately working on this particular problem, I began to see that people are not watching me, that they are involved with their own lives and have very little curiosity about a perfect stranger. Now at long last I can mingle with a strange crowd and feel invisible, enjoy looking and listening to others without fear that I appear pitiful to them. This feeling invisible is one of the greatest gifts of maturity.

My parents separated when I was five and from then on my childhood was spent in various people's homes, sometimes with strangers. The year I lived with Aunt L was a dreary one. Aunt L was a good person and kind to me in her way, but she was a business woman with no real interest in nor time for a small girl. I remember playing with other children on the block one day. Something I said was misunderstood by another little girl. "Ooooh!" she exclaimed, wide-eyed, "You said a dirty word!" I realized instantly which four-letter word it sounded like and I was properly horrified. In those days little middle-class girls never pronounced the words bad little boys scrawled on fences. I hastened to correct her dreadful error and went on to protest vehemently, "My aunt would wash out my mouth with soap if I ever dared say that!" This was a downright lie. Aunt L never listened to anything I said and was certainly not sufficiently interested in me to discipline me for anything I might do. I wanted desperately to be like other kids with mothers who cared. I wanted to belong to a real family. I was ashamed of being a lonely little boarder.

Those who suffer the neurotic fear of loneliness are compulsively busy. They fritter away their time and energy with boring people and meaningless activities. They drown themselves in television or books, forever frustrated and unfulfilled.

For descriptions of *real loneliness* read Moustakas [20], Alfred Kazan's moving portrayal of the agonizing *loneliness* of the stutterer [18], and the description of the loneliness of mental illness by Hannah Greene [19]. *Real loneliness* is part of the human condition, a fact of life. If you are blessed with love and friendship you may not feel it often in your life. But basically, each of us is alone, shut up in our individual skins. Even those who love us can never truly know and share another's suffering. The best we can do is reach out to one another across the abyss that separates us.

The psychological task of adolescence, separation from one's parents, is an experience of intense loneliness. Halfway between the dependence of childhood and the self-reliance of adulthood, the young person dares to step out into the void and try to be himself. Some young people lack the courage to stay with this loneliness and they go through the outward motions of growing up while avoiding the essential step of separation. Some of them remain psychologically stunted all their lives because of this avoidance; others go through a belated adolescence decades later, "breaking free" of people to whom they unconsciously relate as parents. Unfortunately, these new parent figures are frequently marriage partners and the middle-aged "adolescent's" struggle deprives his children of emotional security.

Each of us has at least one opportunity in life to know true loneliness. If we can break free of the neurotic fear and dare to experience it, loneliness can be a creative thing. If we can stop lying to ourselves and dare to feel our true humanness, the pain of loneliness can be therapeutic, with long-lasting, valuable effects on our characters.

Julie was a child of a broken home. Only her grandmother gave her the love and security she craved. When the old lady died suddenly, Julie's world narrowed down to a dark place where no friends could penetrate. A truant from high school, she roamed the city streets for weeks, imprisoned in her loneliness. That agonizing time enriched her. Julie developed a life-long gift of sympathy and warmth for lonely people.

I lost my family when I was in kindergarten. I was so starved for stories that I could hardly wait for first grade to learn to read. There was no one at home then to take an interest in my school work. I envied friends with mothers who made a fuss over them, but I know now in one sense those lonely years were rewarding. My rapid progress in learning to read was uncontaminated by adult praise: no one cared whether I learned or not. I read for fun then and I read for fun today. I turned to books for comfort in those lonely years and books are still a source of strength and joy.

I was in my middle twenties when my stepmother died and I mourned her for half a year. (Years later in self therapy I recognized that on a hidden level I was belatedly mourning the desertion of my natural mother decades earlier.) All those months I was trapped in a bleak loneliness which no loving friend could penetrate, obsessed with the frailty of human life and the impermanence of human relationships. I would never marry, I decided, never become emotionally dependent on anyone, never suffer this kind of loss again. I would control my fate.

At last I came out of that black period, eventually married, and settled down to live happily ever after. But the period of intense loneliness taught me certain truths which have served as guidelines in my life. I realized that life is uncertain, that I can never entirely control my fate. All I can do is put one foot in front of the other and live in the present. My stepmother died at the age of forty-four, having frittered away rare talents and a fine intellect through years of neurotic inertia. I resolved to make use of all my abilities and live life to the full, never to waste any of my precious days on earth. I am fifty-three now and still exploring my latent capacities for work and pleasure, still eager to get my money's worth from life so that I need never look back and regret my wasted years as I regret hers.

When I married I still suffered from the old phobia about loss. I lived in dread that Bernie might die before me. It seemed to me I could not live without him and I hoped he would wait until the children were grown and no longer needed me so I could afford to commit suicide. I watched carefully over his health. Any time he was unexpectedly late from work I panicked (reliving the day I prepared supper and my stepmother failed to come home alive). I hovered over him like a mother hen and, since he is a good sport and tolerant of my neurotic tendencies, Bernie did his best to reassure me he had every intention of living to a ripe old age.

Then I went to that five-day workshop with Fritz. For five days I suffered in my own private hell of loneliness. No one there understood what was happening to me. I could not confide in anyone. Bernie phoned to ask how I was and all I could do was say, "Fine," and cut the conversation short. He seemed so far away, in another world. I knew he could not help me. I realized then with a shock of surprise that for the first time in all the years of our marriage, I had not thought of him while we were apart. I was engulfed in a loneliness that his image could not penetrate. I tried to imagine the time when I would go home again and feel safe and close to him but it seemed as if I were fated to stay here, lonely forever.

LONELINESS

That terrible fantasy did not materialize. For a time after I got home I carried the loneliness with me and could not experience his warmth and love. Then I came out of it and all was as before with one important change. That terrible loneliness had accomplished something for us. I had survived those five days without Bernie. I had taken a giant step forward. I was no longer the helpless Child dreading a Parent's desertion. For the first time I could feel pure Adult love, uncontaminated by need and fear. The phobia of loss was gone and I could be a true partner instead of a responsibility.

Part of my job involves carrying around other people's terrible secrets. Sometimes I have found myself thinking obsessively about some of those private horrors and have noticed myself warding off depression. With self therapy I felt the hidden emotion: loneliness. The burden of other people's tragedies, my helplessness to spare them suffering, must be borne alone. But the years of this professional loneliness, one of the most painful aspects of my work, has strengthened me. Today I am more accepting, less judgmental than I ever dreamed I could be.

15. THE PSYCHOLOGICAL TASKS OF ADOLESCENCE

THOSE WHO have a greater than average capacity for emotional and intellectual growth will take longer to reach maturity. For them psychological adolescence extends into the twenties [22].

There are three stages in human growth: childhood, adolescence and adulthood. We must successfully complete the tasks belonging to each of the first two stages before we can move on to the next.

The task of *childhood* is learning to trust [23]; of *adolescence* to free oneself from dependence on parents and find one's own identity. The true *adult* is self-reliant, self-accepting and accepting of others. The adolescent's task has three aspects:

1. *To fall out of love with his parents*

"It's not fair," my little girl once complained, "you got to marry Daddy, but I'll have to marry a stranger." The adolescent must fall out of love with his parents in order to free himself to love a stranger. He must pull away from the first people he loved before he can achieve intimacy with others.

One symptom of this change is his judgmental attitude toward his parents. I was proud of my stepmother when I was small; she was so charming and witty. Then in adolescence I was ashamed to be seen with her in public; she blew her nose so loud, like a trumpet! Each of my daughters went through some adolescent years when they hated to go anywhere with me. They were ashamed of the clothes I wore ("So undignified!"), ashamed because I walked too fast, laughed too heartily, talked too loud (*"Mommy,* everybody's looking at us!").

It is painful for parents to suddenly know their children are ashamed of them. It is even more painful for the children: they feel guilty about their shame. It would help both if they realized we can only be ashamed of people we love. The fact that we are ashamed of them means we love them. (See "Shame and Guilt" [4]).

The adolescent pulls away from the old intimacy. "My daughter used to confide in me, tell me everything, but now she's so secretive." "Dad and I used to have such good talks together but somehow that's all gone now." Parents who over-react to this rejection, by blackmailing their youngsters with guilt, make adolescence more difficult. Sometimes these children have to resort to deceit: "I talk to my mother just enough to give her the impression I'm confiding in her, but actually I never tell her anything really important about myself."

2. *To fight his own dependency*

The adolescent has one foot in the security of childhood and the other out in the dangerous, unknown void, groping toward independence. There is a part of him that longs to stay in that old, safe place a little longer, at the same time that he is struggling toward self-reliance. He is ashamed of his dependency so sometimes he hides it from himself by projecting it on his parents. "You're over-protective. You won't let me lead my own life. Stop trying to control me." Parents who are genuinely trying to let go may be hurt and resentful at accusations which seem to have no foundation in fact.

The child needs love and approval from his parents. The adolescent is still struggling with some of those needs and he is afraid they will hold him back In order to prove to himself and his parents that he has outgrown them he may act in frightening ways: daring, impulsive, wilful.

The youngster who had to work too hard to maintain love and approval in childhood has learned techniques for handling his parents: appeasing, lying, manipulating, disguising his true thoughts and feelings. Because of that early deprivation his old needs are still unfulfilled and he has great difficulty overcoming them in adolescence. He may postpone performance of this essential task—some neurotics delay adolescence until middle age—or he may spend all his life appeasing, manipulating, lying, dependent on others' love and approval, stuck at the childhood level in all his relationships.

An extremely deprived child will over-react to his hidden dependency in adolescence by denying it in an exaggerated way. He compulsively acts out negative feelings toward his parents and all authority figures—arrogant, rebellious, punishing, degrading—and may never grow beyond that stage. Unconsciously he hates his hidden dependency, consciously he hates the parents with whom those feelings are involved. The child who received *no love or approval at all* in childhood, who never learned to trust, becomes a psychopath [10].

3. *To find his identity*

The small child sees himself as a member of his family: the child of his parents, the sibling of other children in the household. In adolescence he must free himself from that old self-image and find a new one; he must discover his individuality. Now he begins to break away from the family's ways but he is not yet ready to know his own way. In this transition between childhood and adulthood he needs a temporary identity, a self-image to tide him over while he is casting off old ways. He latches on to someone else's life style for the time being: an admired adult (not his parents), a friend, a peer group, perhaps an author or literary character. The parent who sneers at his youngster's apparently slavish conformity to the clothes and manners of his crowd, does not understand that the adolescent is only borrowing a new identity, trying it on for size in an effort to discover his own.

Some parents make such a fuss about trivia that both they and their youngsters are misled into treating a foolish skirmish as if it were a significant battle. A mother who overevaluates the importance of dress or hair style will encourage her son to focus his thoughts and efforts on the struggle about personal appearance. He expends so much energy on this superficial problem that he neglects the real task of adolescence: discovering his place in the world, his approach to life. Mother and son are kidding themselves; both cherish the illusion that he is performing an essential task of adolescence. Meanwhile precious time and energy needed for genuine growth are frittered away in mock battles.

To reach adulthood, the individual must discard some of his family's ways and develop new ones. In adolescence he may appear to be throwing out the baby with the bath; discarding *all* their standards, deliberately doing the opposite of what they want. In general, people retain meaningful values from their parents, although this may not be apparent during the years of adolescent turmoil. Some parents panic during this time and try harder to impose their ideas on their children. In an attempt to avoid feeling helpless,these parents become tougher, more authoritarian at an age when the young person needs more freedom than ever before in his life. This desperate attempt to control merely aggravates the adolescent's rebellion, giving it real justification. It also widens the gulf between them, sometimes beyond healing. Frantic parents who turn to the police for help at this time set themselves up as their child's enemy, to be feared and distrusted forever after.

When you turn your child over to a law enforcement agency, when you subject him to the degrading and frightening experience of imprisonment, you give him the self-image of a criminal. Friedenberg [24] describes how we categorize young people. Just at the time of his life when he is groping for his identity, our society puts him in a box. His behavior is labeled in clear-cut terms: well-adjusted, sick (neurotic) or delinquent; there is no room in between for individual variation, no recognition of conflicting urges, no acceptance of adolescence as a transitional, experimental period. The tragedy is that the young person accepts this label and resigns himself to his fate.

Some parents try to control with emotional blackmail—guilt: "You're breaking your mother's heart." "You're giving your father a heart attack." "I'm going to have a nervous breakdown." If they fail to sabotage the adolescent's growth, they sow seeds for lifetime resentment. Others use more direct threats: "While I'm supporting you, you'll do things my way." "I wash my hands of you." "You are no son of mine."

Today especially, when a whole generation is experimenting with drugs and the hippy way of life, some hysterical parents act out their offsprings' worst fantasies of rejection and abandonment. They push them into permanent decisions at a time when they need to experiment with new ideas, try out new ways of behavior, grope for a life style and personal philosophy. Instead of giving the young adult time to face his own inner conflict between dependence and independence, he is encouraged to experience the problem as a power struggle between Parent and Child. This either greatly delays the growth toward adulthood or stops it entirely, so that he remains forever at the stage of adolescent rebellion.

The adolescent must find his sexual identity. The small boy in our culture, surrounded by women at home and at school, may have little opportunity to identify with a male. He may reach adolescence with a confused sexual self image which frightens him and he knows that our culture degrades, punishes, and at best ghettoizes male homosexuals.

The little girl who was taught to compete with boys in school suddenly finds that she is expected to be seductive, not competitive. Everything in the culture and the mass media combines to threaten her self esteem if she fails to attract males.

The parent who is eager to help his young adult with good advice about appearance and public behavior should remember that this is an age when he is tormented by self-doubt. Almost any such comment feeds into that inner voice that keeps telling him how ugly and/or inadequate he is.

The adolescent is trying to find his work role in the world. Unlike boys in simpler societies, most sons miss the opportunity to help their fathers and learn the male skills which they expect to practice in adulthood. They have very little real knowledge of their father's jobs. In a mechanized society the opportunities for satisfying work are limited, this complicates the adolescent's problems in finding his work identity [24], [25].

The girl is given educational opportunities and encouraged to consider her potential for creative work at the same time that she receives the subtle but powerful message to focus on her ability to get a man to the exclusion of all other interests.

Helena Deutsch [26] says that to the extent to which a woman has unresolved problems about her relationship with her own mother, she will have difficulty understanding and accepting her daughter in adolescence. This is equally true for fathers. Hidden feelings about our parents, alive or dead, blur our vision. Left-over fear, anger, jealousy, dependency needs, distort our thinking and contaminate our relationships with our adolescents.

The generation gap has existed between parent and child since time immemorial, but it may be wider today than ever before. Within the memory of living man, history has moved so rapidly, the upheaval of time-honored institutions and mores has been so radical, that our young adults see the world very differently from the way we and their grandparents did. The adolescent has always tended to discard some of his parents' values, but today's children label our whole way of life meaningless. A generation of depression-traumatized, security-minded parents see young people of an affluent society ignore dire warnings and sneer at middle-class values. No wonder parents are frightened, judgmental and frantic [30].

Another factor widening the generation gap is the modern child-centered home. We who were brought up in old-fashioned, authoritarian homes where children were supposed to be seen but not heard, swung over to Gisell and Ilg, Dr. Spock, and the whole permissive child-rearing school. We taught our children to feel and express their emotions, to demand their rights. While you may not feel threatened when your four-year-old stamps his little foot and screams, "You're a mean mommy and I hate you!", if he continues along these lines when he has grown taller, physically stronger, and more articulate than you, it's hard to keep your cool. My own experiences in self-therapy revealed that often when one of my adolescent children expressed negative feelings toward me, underneath my apparent anger something very different was hidden.

GESTALT SELF THERAPY

Here are some of the hidden emotions I discovered from time to time in self therapy:

I was over-identifying with my child. I myself had never dared express anger toward parents in my childhood and by the time I was an adolescent, under the thumb of a rigid and controlling stepmother whom I loved and feared, I had accumulated a tremendous backlog of rage. This I managed to control by a terrible effort of will accompanied by obsessive thoughts of suicide as my unchanneled anger turned inward. When my adolescent daughter was irritated with me I assumed she was hating me with the same intensity I felt toward my stepmother.

One year I announced to my adult class that the next week's lecture would be on adolescence, and young people were invited to sit in. As the day of the lecture approached I began to suffer anxiety. I dreaded getting up there in front of all those teen-agers. They would be bound to hate me; I was a parent and a teacher—the enemy, and what could I possibly tell them that they would want to hear, that would sound useful to them? In desperation I phoned my younger daughter who had been living away from home for some time. I asked her for advice. What would have been helpful to her at that age? "Remember that last year you lived at home when you were hating me all the time?", I began. She sounded shocked. "Mommy! I never hated you. It's true you bugged me a lot." She laughed a little. "And, I used to feel annoyed with you at peculiar times. If I bumped my elbow on the door jamb going from one room to another I'd feel a flash of irritation at you as if it was all your fault, but I always knew that was irrational right away."

That was an enormous relief. Even in recent years when gestalt self therapy and communication with my children has made me more aware of the stupid and neurotic things I did to them and their real justification for annoyance, it helps to remember her words, "I never hated you." I am still so haunted by my stepmother that an irrational part of me feels that I am just like her and that I deserve my children's hatred, while another part of me over-identifies with my angry daughter. Today, in gestalt self therapy, I am working through my old rage toward my stepmother. How I wish I had learned to do that when my girls still lived at home.

The young person pursuing his developmental task of falling out of love with his parents and freeing himself from his dependence on them is often critical and judgmental. The father who was once the object of his child's admiration, accustomed to overhearing bits of conversation like, "But my daddy says . . ." in tones of perfect faith, is now in for a painful jolt. Mothers too begin to hear, "Oh, mommy!" in that despairing tone which translated means, "You don't know anything at all!"

If you find yourself over-reacting to this new attitude, you may discover in self therapy that you are unconsciously reversing roles: acting as if you are the scolded child and your adolescent the disapproving parent. After you have felt this hidden material you will be able once again to experience yourself as an adult and accept your child's criticism more comfortably.

Each parent reacts to this new relationship out of his personal history. When my children began to cast disapproving glances at me I regressed to my own early years. Once more I felt like a foster child, living on the fringes of other people's families, unloved, unwanted, barely tolerated.

Sometimes the hidden feeling is envy of all this new freedom we never had as described in "Envy and Jealousy."

Sometimes it is the simple inability to step down from the old role of helpful parent. The child to whom parents' and teachers' approval was once all-important, is now concerned with the acceptance of his peers. The establishment, once his pillar of support, has suddenly become the enemy. This change of attitude is a horrid surprise to parents and some of them, refusing to face the truth, continue futilely to use the same old threats and bribes that once worked, and are now worse than useless, to control their adolescents.

Adolescence is a time of stress and strain for child and parent alike. The less flexible and more rigid they both are, the more traumatic this period will be for both.

16. ENVY & JEALOUSY

ENVY. Webster's definition of envy: "painful or resentful awareness of an advantage enjoyed by another joined with a desire to possess the same advantage."

Most of us experience pangs of envy once in a while, but for some unfortunate people envy is a poison that seeps through every experience and contaminates all areas of their lives. Chronically envious people are those who long ago learned to see themselves as inadequate human beings [12]. How did they acquire this self image? Two kinds of parent-child relationships produce envious people:

a) Parents who are dissatisfied with their child, expect him to have greater gifts of beauty, intelligence, talent or whatever qualities they tend to overevaluate. He is convinced, all his life, that he does not rate.

b) Parents who have an irrational, extravagant picture of their child, an unreal, exaggerated idea of his gifts. No matter how ambitious he is, no matter how hard he works, he can never realistically prove to the world that he is capable of the achievements his parents predicted for him. He can never attain their excessively high goals.

The chronically envious person is constantly preoccupied with the gain or loss of prestige. All kinds of accomplishment and possessions seem, in his eyes, to have glamour which can give him status. Since he is convinced that he has very little of his own to begin with, he believes he must accumulate all these marks of prestige in order to be merely equal with others. He has to keep trying to convince the world that he is not inferior.

Many envious people, because of this all-pervasive insecurity, are more relaxed on vacation, in a new place with people who are strangers and do not fit into any special competitive category. But if they stay in the same vacation resort too long, and get to know these people well enough to measure themselves against them, they are then compelled

ENVY AND JEALOUSY

to impress them.

Envy is a very unpleasant emotion. It has two painful aspects:

a) Our culture frowns on envy. It is a religious sin to covet your neighbor's possessions. We are ashamed of feeling envy and expect others to feel disapproval and disgust.

b) When you envy someone, you are painfully aware that he has the ability to get things you cannot. Since the envious person is convinced of his own inferiority, his own inability to get things, each pang of envy, comparing himself with another, rubs salt in the wound.

The envious person justifies his resentment of the other's good fortune by criticizing him. He invents all kinds of irrational explanations to vindicate himself: "It's unfair; if there were any justice I would have those things instead; he is undeserving, dishonest, bad, etc."

Certain aspects of our culture encourage envy. Americans have difficulty achieving intimacy and alienation breeds envy. The tremendous development of our natural resources, mass production, and advertising urge us to value things for their prestige value. Keeping up with the Jones' is a way of life.

American parents teach their children to disparage others. Little Susie comes home crying because Mary called her "fatso". Mother rushes to the rescue with a barefaced lie: "Mary is so skinny, I'd worry if she were my little girl. You don't have to pay attention to what she says, dear." And little Susie learns to distrust her own observation and to pervert the truth in order to feel more comfortable.

This tendency of the chronically envious person to distort reality is dangerous. It can develop into a paranoid attitude. If you recognize that you feel envy frequently, use your self awareness for self therapy and avoid growing more irrational. Any emotion which you feel very frequently is what I call a *stereotyped reaction*, a blanket cover to hide all kinds of feelings. A stereotyped reaction is always material for self therapy, no matter how reasonable and appropriate it seems to you. Each time you peel away a layer of envy and feel what lies underneath—inadequacy, worthlessness, helplessness, etc.—you move on toward health and avoid more serious illness.

In gestalt self therapy, have an imaginary encounter with the person you envy. Accuse him of all the bad things you have thought of him—his unworthiness, his wickedness. Scold him. Tell him why he does not deserve this good fortune, then play the part of that "worthless" person. Next play both parts of yourself; the side that thinks you deserve all those "important" things versus the side that feels undeserving of them. As you learn how much of your own hidden conviction of worthlessness you project on envied people, you will begin to grow.

Those of us who are not chronically envious, for whom envy is not a stereotyped reaction, also envy from time to time. Envy is always an inappropriate reaction, a cover for some hidden feeling. After my mother left me when I was five years old, I envied other children, children with normal homes and loving mothers. Even as an adult I used to feel a pang of envy whenever I heard someone complain about an overprotective mother. I have done a great deal of self therapy on my hidden feelings about my mother, about being a foster child, being "different". In recent years that envy has disappeared and I can recognize that the person who had an overprotective, controlling, smothering mother may have had a harder time than I.

When I was a small girl in elementary school I was obsessed with envy of a classmate. I bitterly resented her popularity, her scholastic success and her lively, attractive style. For years my bed-time prayer was, "Please God, let me beat May Bright." I focused on May Bright and my envy of her in order to avoid feeling lonely and rejected, a mere foster child.

Envy helps you to concentrate on the other person. It distracts you from what is going on inside yourself. Envy is always a cover for some other feeling, good material for self therapy.

Years ago, before I had any professional status in the community, I was starved for audiences. Like a true missionary, I lectured to any group that would listen to me. I offered my services, free, to a certain local organization which regularly invited weekly speakers on various subjects. The program chairman accepted my offer gratefully, but next day she phoned apologetically. She explained that she was new on the job and her superiors had scolded her for going over their heads to invite a speaker; the lecture was cancelled. In those days I was considered a maverick in my field and I knew certain members of the board objected to my off-beat approach to psychology: they thought I was a quack. So I accepted what was only one more setback to my missionary zeal and went on to find other audiences.

Some months later I read an announcement in the local paper to the effect that this same organization which had rejected me was presenting a course with a title similar to the one I used, given by a local psychologist. I was eaten up with envy and suffered obsessive thinking and depression. After a few miserable days I used my writing technique [4] for self therapy to get some relief.

This method consists of writing down questions, guesses about your hidden feeling, until a new emotion pops up, more intense than the apparent one with which you began. It is not designed to analyze yourself intellectually, only to open the door to a hidden feeling. Some of your guesses will sound reasonable, but unless it stimulates an intense feeling, you drop it and try another idea on for size. In order to get beneath the envy I wrote:

How do I feel about this course? Depressed. What am I afraid to feel? Disappointed? Angry? Competitive? Do I feel left out? Is it the foster child again? Nobody appreciates me? Is this jealousy of the "real" children in the family? Anger at the grown-ups who don't recognize or care? [These were old self therapy insights.] What am I afraid to feel? Why is this so painful that I'm frozen? My teeth beginning to ache. How did I feel when I first read it? Dr. -------. Do I feel he's stealing something from me? Desire to eat. Trying to distract myself with reading Maslow [intellectualizing]. What am I afraid to feel? Fear? Loss of faith in my work? Am I dependent on their approval? Afraid if they don't recognize me I'm nothing? Afraid to continue working, as if I

175

have nothing real to say? As if I'm not real? Like Sara Crewe [a novel from childhood] pretending to be a princess when I'm only a foster child? Afraid I'm a phony because they think I am? Because I lied about my family? [Pretended my stepmother was my real mother.] Tried to belong, be like other children. Ashamed of learning from experience (crying). Is that what experience means? Sex experience. Learned from life instead of books. [Traumatic childhood sex experience.] Ashamed. As if they are accusing me. Not like other children. Pretending to be.

I felt that shame intensely. It only lasted a few seconds. When I finished, the envy, the depression and the obsessive thinking disappeared. The whole thing seemed unimportant and I could let go of it.

Our culture, which stimulates envy, at the same time labels it shameful and so some of us learn to avoid feeling it. We hide envy with other feelings. Years ago, in one of my first workshops, a student shamefacedly confessed that she envied another member because she was so pretty. Most of the group assured her that they could easily identify with her, that they too suffered envy from time to time. My chief reaction was surprise and I blurted out, "I never envy anybody".

After the session, I thought about that. I was suspicious of myself, since my announcement was uncalled for, nontherapeutic, and out of character for me. Here was a student who had dared to admit what was to her a shameful experience and while the group members immediately reassured here, I the leader, had burst out with a remark she might well have taken to be unsympathetic and superior.

That was an inappropriate reaction, self-defeating in terms of my own standards for leadership, a clue that I was hiding something from myself.

That was Step 1 in self therapy. Recognize an inappropriate reaction (Appendix I). Step 2, feel the apparent emotion. I went back to the incident, felt again the surprise to learn that envy was such a common emotion. Step 3. What else did I feel? A general desire to talk that student out of feelings, to prove to her she did not have to feel envy. Step 4. What did this remind me of? And then I remembered (with a shock at my capacity for self-deception) envy I had only recently outgrown. For several years I envied a certain tall (I am all of five feet) glamorous woman who had acquired enormous prestige from the general public and respectful recognition from the profession for her original work in psychology.

People were forever telling me that her lectures were just as stimulating and entertaining as mine. They usually said this with a look of expectant delight as if they were sure I'd love to hear it, and I always wanted to hit them.

For years I flinched whenever I heard her name or read glowing accounts of her accomplishments. At long last, by dint of hard work in self therapy, I outgrew that degrading envy, but my newfound freedom was accompanied by a kind of amnesia for the whole experience. I had carefully forgotten all about it. When, however, I dared to remember and admit my weakness, I could be a more useful workshop leader, not only accepting, but truly understanding of envious people.

There are many ways to cover up envy and disguise it with other emotions. My first child was always starved for stories, and as soon as she was old enough, became an avid reader like me. I made my weekly visits to the library while she was at school, and in addition to my own books, always brought home an armful for her.

At first she enjoyed my choices, but as the years went by she began to develop her individual tastes and I could not always be sure what she wanted, so I picked out an assortment from which she could choose. That seemed to work out nicely. One day when Jeanie was inspecting the latest collection, choosing those she liked, she complained, "Oh, Mommy, why do you get books I don't like?"

I was filled with righteous indignation, so furious I could not trust myself to speak. I left the room and just let myself rage silently. ("Spoiled brat! She doesn't deserve such a good mother. What other mother goes to the library every single week and spends so much time trying to satisfy her child's tastes? How can she be so unappreciative when I'm so good to her?") Finally it occurred to me that I might be hiding something from myself. That was Step 1, recognize an inappropriate or too painful emotion. Step 2, feel the apparent emotion. I felt judgmental of my daughter's ingratitude. Step 3. What did I feel just before the apparent emotion? Disappointed. I had expected her to be happy. When I chose books for Jeanie I looked forward to her enjoyment with the same anticipation as baking pies for Bernie. I experienced a vicarious pleasure in their satisfaction. Step 4. What did this remind me of? How wonderful it would have seemed to me as a child if I had someone to bring books home for me. Then I went back to my childhood; to my dependence on books; my desperate need to escape into stories; my sadistic foster mother who destroyed my library card as punishment so that I had to read and reread the same few books the two years I lived with her. I re-lived that starved feeling and then I realized what lay under my indignation—envy. The deprived child within me was envious of my daughter's riches.

As soon as I felt that hidden envy, which lasted only a few moments, the apparent emotion, the righteous indignation, evaporated and, as usually happens after self therapy, the Adult began to function. I went inside and told Jeanie, "It's silly for me to be picking out books for you. From now on, I'll wait till you come home from school and I'll take you to the library. You're getting to be a big girl now and you have a perfect right to choose your own books." Jeanie was delighted and from then on there was no more book trouble. I am still ashamed to realize how I had deprived her of that right. Hidden feelings do strange things to our intellects.

When my younger daughter was in her teens she went to a youth group meeting one evening. One of the parents drove her, and Bernie and I went to sleep. Eventually we were awakened by the sound of a car driving up. Ann came into our room and asked, "Is it OK if I sleep at Mary's house?" We said, "Yes", assuming that the same car was waiting outside for her. Suddenly we heard the garage door opening. We lay there for a few moments trying to figure out what that meant. By the time we realized Ann was taking her bike out of the garage, she had gone. She was not being driven to

ENVY AND JEALOUSY

Mary's house. She was biking there, late at night, *with no bicycle light.* That was strictly against our rules as she well knew. It appeared to us as if she had deliberately allowed us to think she was going by car, since she knew we would forbid her to bicycle at that hour. Bernie was furious. He jumped out of bed, pulled his trousers on over his pajamas; I threw a coat over my nightgown; and we were off to the races! He was going to follow her in the car and demand that she come home with us immediately. The trouble was, although we knew where Mary lived, we could not know which route Ann would take to get there. So there we were in our prowl car, cruising up and down every street in the neighborhood while honest citizens were safe in bed. No bike in sight. Eventually we arrived at Mary's house and there was Ann's bike parked in front. Bernie went to tell Ann to come home. Since she had already arrived, and since I dreaded the clash of wills between them, I waited in the car while he went forth to battle. After a while Bernie came out and said sheepishly, "You'd better come in and see what you can do. I can't budge her and I don't understand what's going on." It was the first time a child of ours had deliberately disobeyed him openly, simply said "No" to an order, and he was shaken.

I followed him inside and there we were confronted by a whole roomful of young people who simply stood there behind Ann, looking at us. No one spoke, no one showed any expression whatsoever. It was like a bad dream and I felt absolutely helpless. I don't remember what I said, but I laughed and tried to lighten the atmosphere a little and make the showdown seem less dramatic. I asked, "What is going on?" and Ann quietly but firmly said, "Daddy wants me to come home and I don't want to." Obviously we could not forcibly remove her and obviously nothing else was going to move her, so Bernie and I did our best to save face and left gracefully.

Bernie had a bad night. He was hurt that Ann would defy him publicly that way. He thought she deliberately humiliated him in front of her friends. Next morning at breakfast he was still upset. What about me? Well, I was sorry he had stuck his neck out that way, that he had rushed after her so impulsively and set himself up for a battle he was bound to lose. I hated seeing him hurt and wished I had been able to spare him. How did I feel about Ann? Nothing. I felt cold, detached as if she were a stranger. I kept saying, "We give her so much freedom and she's not satisfied. She has to flaunt her power and deliberately hurt you. I can't understand it."

But the coldness frightened me. She was my child and I had always loved her. What was happening to me? There must be something I was hiding from myself, something underneath that coldness. That was Step 1, Recognize an inappropriate emotion. Step 2. Feel the apparent emotion. All I felt was absence of emotion—coldness, alienation from my own child. Step 3. What did I feel just before the apparent emotion? I was filled with righteous indignation: How ungrateful she was after all the freedom we gave her. We had spoiled her. She couldn't appreciate what she had, etc. Step 4. What does this remind me of? All that freedom! *I* never had it so good! At her age homelife with my stepmother was like a reform school. I lived by the clock, each moment of my day accounted for, no nights out during the week and strict, early curfew on weekends. I lived in dread of my stepmother's rage at the smallest infraction of her countless rules.

Suddenly I knew what the hidden feeling was—envy. It was as simple as that: I envied my teen-age daughter the freedom I had so desperately craved in my girlhood. So I let myself feel that envy and the shame that went with it (it is degrading to feel envious of your own child for whom you want the best) and then it evaporated. The coldness, the feeling of separation from my daughter was gone too. Instead I felt simple curiosity. "I don't know what was in Ann's mind last night," I told Bernie, "But it isn't like her to deliberately hurt or humiliate anyone, especially her father. She'll be home soon and we'll ask her." (Until then I had not wanted to talk to her at all.)

And that is what we did. She walked in while we were still at the breakfast table and sat down with us. "What happened last night, Annie?" I asked her. Bernie said, "Did you have to humiliate me in front of all your friends?" Well, it turned out that she hated hurting him and had not wanted to.

180

ENVY AND JEALOUSY

"I was just terribly, terribly depressed last night, more than I've ever been," she explained, "I knew I had to be with my friends at any cost. Yes, I knew you wouldn't let me go if I didn't have a car ride, so I didn't tell you I was going to bike there. I never deliberately want to hurt either of you, but sometimes I have to do things that I know are right for me that you can't understand, even if it means hurting you. I don't do things to hurt you but I do them in spite of the fact they may hurt you." That was the most important message I ever received from a young adult and I never forgot it. It has stood me in good stead many times when I was tempted to interpret their behavior as purposely directed against me. Our children are mainly concerned with growing up, finding themselves, and sometimes our feelings get in the way. They cannot afford to slow up their progress in order to protect us. Not that this information stops me from feeling hurt time and time again, but at least my intellect can remember and push me into self therapy to explore the hurt.

Incidentally, we told Ann we would prefer to get out of bed and drive her if she needed that desperately to go somewhere, rather than have her bicycle late at night.

The moral of this story is that my hidden envy, disguised as coldness, would have blocked any real communication between Ann and me and blown the whole incident up to ominous proportions. In recent years I have often peeled away that layer of envy. In gestalt self therapy the hidden feelings are sometimes rage and frustration toward my stepmother; sometimes shame at having been so obedient and cowardly in my youth.

I notice that in both these cases of hidden envy toward my children, I felt judgmental. I wonder how much of the "generation gap" comes from hidden envy of young people for what we older people missed.

JEALOUSY, jealous: "intolerant of rivalry or unfaithfulness; disposed to suspect rivalry or unfaithfulness; apprehensive of the loss of another's exclusive devotion; hostile toward a rival." -Webster's definition.

Harry Stack Sullivan says that next to anxiety, jealousy is the most painful emotion a human being can feel. It is acute, dramatic and devasting. If you are not sure what jealousy feels like, read Proust's description [13].

A person who suffers *often* from jealousy is one who cannot experience complete intimacy with another person. He is incapable of unique satisfaction with any one person. He fantasizes that the person he loves can have greater satisfaction with a third person, that these other two people can be happier with one another than he can ever be.

Basically, deep down on a hidden level, he is convinced of his own unworthiness in comparison with his rival. He also believes that he does not deserve the person he loves, that the loved one is better than he is and has greater capacity than he, that he is not up to the level of people he cares for.

Most of us have had some experience with jealousy. When I was small, I was jealous of my foster sister. My foster mother loved her, not me. In my first gestalt workshop with Fritz Perls I regressed to that Child level and was bitterly jealous of the other women Fritz liked instead of me, and a most humiliating experience that was, to feel jealousy of the "other children" at my age.

In the early years of my marriage I suffered pangs of jealousy each time Bernie said something nice about another woman. I was used to my father, who often made disparaging remarks about women. He looked at them with a critical eye—they were too fat or too thin, too plain or too heavily made-up, etc. But Bernie likes women. He can always find something attractive in any female. In those days several factors contributed to make me doubt my ability to have a good marriage: the war kept us apart the first year; both my parents had failed dramatically and frequently in marriage. A symptom of my insecurity was jealousy. I used to keep an eye out for any possible rivals, though Bernie has never been flirtatious. Like my father, I would carefully point out the bad points of young women we came across. "How self-conscious and affected she is" I might (truthfully) observe, and Bernie would immediately come to her defense: "But she's so young!" "How plain she is." "But she's very graceful." Each time this happened I would feel ashamed of my nastiness and annoyed that I had made him focus his attention on the girl. Eventually I learned to keep my mouth shut and suffer in silence.

I have not felt that jealousy for many years. My guess is that when I realized I was capable of a deep, intimate relationship, I stopped worrying about competitors.

Obsessive jealousy is always material for self therapy. As with envy, apparent emotion focusses on the *other person* as a means of warding off painful feelings about yourself: inability to compete, inadequacy in human relations, lack of genuine intimacy, worthlessness. Sometimes jealousy hides confusion about one's sexual identity. You may find that you are over-identifying with the person you love. If you are a woman, for example, you may over-identify with the man you love. Your hidden thought may be, "Of course he loves her. She is so attractive. How can he help it? I'm attracted to her myself."

If you suffer extreme, obsessive jealousy a great deal in your life, it is important to explore it in self therapy. Do not let yourself stay with the apparent emotion too long. The danger in focusing on others in jealousy instead of getting down to your own hidden feelings, is similar to the danger in chronic envy. You begin to destroy reality to fit in with your fantasy. This can develop into paranoia.

Here is an example of how jealousy made me distort reality and of how I used it for self therapy. Years ago, when I was teaching self therapy in three different school districts, one of the principals, who had never heard me lecture and was not interested in self therapy, decided at the end of a summer session that I should skip the fall term. "You've been teaching the same course for too many successive terms. I think you've reached the saturation point in this district." Though 15 was the minimum number of students required for a course, I had 50 that summer. A great many of them were eagerly waiting to sign up again for the fall. People who are trying to learn self therapy tend to stay with my classes a long time. Eventually, I learned that people would travel to hear me, and that one school was all I needed. But at that time I was terribly frustrated and irrationally worried about losing that class.

Some time later I read the announcement of a new course to be given in that very school, entitled "Self Analysis." My jealousy of this new teacher who seemed to be taking my place was so intense that I had a mild anxiety attack and turned to the writing technique for self therapy in order to get some relief. This is what I wrote:

> Feel shaky. Trouble breathing. Why? Mr. X [principal] giving a course called Self Analysis has different teacher. I'm jealous? Feel like outsider? Feel like foster child? Jealous of sibling? No. Unfair. Someone is stealing my material but can't possibly give my course. Someone is going to cheat my students. Mr. X in collusion, trying to get some favorite teacher in my place [notice the paranoid distortion]. Why am I so upset? Wish I could cry. Feel frightened. Anxiety symptoms. What am I afraid of? Mr. X doesn't like me. So what? Is he a dangerous adult threatening me? Afraid to be hurt? Feel rejected? Feel like unloved child? Why do I feel so upset? Disappointed? No. Angry? Afraid of my own anger? I hate him but am afraid to hate. My hatred will be turned back on myself. Feel as if father stopped loving me. Lost interest in me. No longer feel I am his child. The way Dad treated me that summer. Still feel shaky. Why? Jealous of other teacher? Who is he? An impostor. Not as good as I am. Someone with prestige or pull. What or who am I jealous of? Reminds me of anger toward fake professionals who don't care about their patients, mislead them, damage them. I care so much (crying now). Why won't they let me teach when I know I can do a real job? Not allowed to work. Not appreciated.

For a few brief moments I stayed with that painful feeling, a feeling more appropriate to my neglected childhood than to the adult I had become; then it was gone. The intense, painful jealousy was gone too. I just didn't care any more. I knew very well that no matter what the new course was entitled, no one else could teach my kind of self therapy because I had invented it, and I began to guess that people who wanted what I had to offer would seek me out.

Since jealousy is the second most painful emotion known to man, some of us will go to great lengths to avoid it, to cover it up with something else. When Shostrum's book, [27]

ENVY AND JEALOUSY

MAN THE MANIPULATOR, came out, with an introduction by Fritz Perls, I could find nothing good about it. In fact I could hardly read it. I criticized and sneered and was appalled when some of my very own students not only liked it, but found it helpful. Eventually I discovered that my critical judgment was distorted by the hidden feeling—jealousy. To my embarrassment I finally recognized that I was bitterly jealous because Fritz had written such a glowing report of Shostrum's book, whereas he never said a word about mine. I was still caught up in my transference on Fritz: to the Child within me, Shostrum was a brother whom Daddy loved more than me. The absurdity of this jealousy and the way it perverted my critical faculties, helped give me the extra push I needed to work on my transference on Fritz and free myself from it.

17. SELF THERAPY WORKSHOPS

WHEN I first read about Synanon [32] a new door opened for me. Dope addicts, society's discards, were learning to live satisfying, productive lives! That meant human beings were more flexible than psychiatry ever dreamed. If these damaged people could change, surely ordinary neurotics could make tremendous strides given the same opportunities.

Synanon provides a family life for dope addicts. They live with others like themselves, lead by a strong, supportive parent figure—not a professional psychotherapist, but someone who has lived through experiences like their own, someone who struggled and made it, someone who can be a model for them. Synanon people live together in the kind of family they missed in childhood, where members can understand and care about one another, where it is safe to be genuinely honest. They are getting a second chance to go back and live through those experiences we all need to give us strength and courage to grow.

I was inspired. I dreamed of giving my students this second chance: a kind of family life with others like themselves and with me, a surrogate parent—not a professional psychotherapist, just another average neurotic who struggled and made it, an ordinary person with experiences like their own who pulled herself up by her bootstraps and is ready to lend a helping hand.

I regret that I cannot take people into my home on a long-term basis, that I cannot give my students the kind of reparenting Jacqui Lee Schiff gives schizophrenics [31]. But the weekend workshops (Appendix III) function like a family and those who are genuinely committed to growth come back time after time. They let themselves experience what their fellow group members have to offer and they begin to change and grow in exciting ways.

Little by little the workshops are changing. Today they are essentially Self Therapy Workshops, a far cry from my

186

original Communication Workshops With Self Therapy Homework [4]. Group members still communicate on a concrete
here-and-now level, but there is less emphasis on handling
others, and more concern with personal growth. They use
workshop encounters in a truly creative way, as material for
on-the-spot self therapy. People are becoming more self-
aware, exploring their own irrational feelings. Instead of
using group feedback for mere intellectual learning, instead
of trying to conform and adjust on a superficial level, they
are changing self-defeating patterns on a gut level.

I used to teach self therapy through lectures and writing.
That was like trying to teach a skill without practical demonstration. Today, in the workshops where the action is, I am
a participating member of the family. From time to time
something stirs up one of my irrational areas and students
can watch me go through the process of self therapy. They
can use me as their model.

I used to use only myself as a guinea pig, as illustrative
material for teaching. Today students learn from one another. Instead of the presentation of only one kind of neurotic, workshops provide a variety of personalities and
self-defeating patterns with which to identify and learn.

Everybody has his own special way of doing self therapy.
I used to teach the method that worked for me. The workshop atmosphere stimulates creativity and group members
evolve their own self therapy techniques. They teach one
another, and me, by example. I learn something new in each
session.

I have learned that we can go further back into the past
than I ever dreamed. Years ago, after decades of self control, self therapy gave me permission to cry but my tears
were always silent and few. I used to shut them off as soon
as they gave me relief from my apparent emotion. Young
adults in workshops surprised me when their voices changed
in self therapy. The sound of crying that sounded appropriate to their age at first, gradually grew younger and younger
as they went deeper into the past. Mothers in the group
recognized the infant screams and had the uncanny feeling
that we had a tiny baby in the room.

I learned that my own self therapy tears were merely

those of the Adult pitying the Child of the past. In gestalt self therapy I began to move further back into my childhood and was surprised to hear myself sobbing like that little girl I once was. Other middle-aged group members are learning from the younger, more flexible ones, that they too can go further back.

Group members reenacting painful scenes from childhood have pushed me into reliving experiences I avoided all my life. They have given me courage to feel hurt and helplessness and primitive fear.

All my life I have been driven by a compulsive need to hurry, haunted by a dread of being late for appointments and in completing work. Although I have longed for freedom from that tormenting voice that nags, "Hurry, hurry," I never gained any long-term results from my old self therapy techniques.

This year I was so troubled by that syndrome that in desperation I tried again. I began by reliving the most recent crisis where I was almost late, and then asked myself, "What will happen if I don't hurry? What dread catastrophe am I always avoiding? When was I too late to avoid catastrophe?"

I remembered my stepmother's death. In the midst of health she was suddenly rushed to the hospital one night with a mysterious pain. When I arrived at the hospital the next morning her room was empty. I ran frantically down the corridor searching for her until a nurse said, "Oh, my God, didn't they tell you? She died last night."

In gestalt self therapy I went back to the long subway ride to the hospital and relived the frantic desire to hurry.

Muriel: Hurry, hurry! Oh, please move faster. I won't get there in time. I have to get there or she'll die.

Train: I won't hurry. I'll hold you back. I won't let you get there in time.

Muriel: (Frantic, tensing every muscle, trying to move the train with her feet). Please, please let me get there. Don't hold me back. She'll die, (etc. with anxiety and frustration).

SELF THERAPY WORKSHOPS

After a while I asked myself, "What else does this remind me of? Who else might have died if I didn't hurry?" Then I recalled stories about the circumstances of my birth. I was born at home and my mother was given no anesthetics. She had little tolerance for pain and was terrified. After twenty-two terrible hours the doctor dragged me out with instruments whose scars I still bear.

It was just a wild guess: I had no feelings about that experience and went into the gestalt in cold blood. I lay down on my side in the fetal position, knees bent. Without planning it, I wrapped my arms around my knees and suddenly found myself struggling desperately to free myself from my tightly clasped hands, trying in vain to straighten my legs.

Muriel: Let me out! Let me out! Please let me out before it's too late.

Mother: I can't let you out. I'm too scared.

Muriel: Please, please. I have to get out or I'll die. Let me live. Let me out.

This went on for some time. I struggled and sobbed and screamed in an unrecognizeable voice. This was the most intense self therapy experience of my life. As always, the Adult sat calmly by, surprised, but the Child was back there struggling in urgency and fear. I came out of it, like most of my workshop people after self therapy, soaking wet with perspiration, physically exhausted, and elated. Since then I am free of that life-long compulsion to hurry. I still move at a brisk clip—that is my life style—but the drivenness, the pressure of urgency, is gone. I enjoy my work. That nagging voice, "Hurry! Hurry!" is gone at last.

Although we have none of the games and exercises in our workshops that are practiced in some groups, props are available for anyone who wants to use them to help channel feelings. I notice that people who fear their own dangerous power prefer to hit pillows in anger. They seem to need reassurance that they have not destroyed their victims: the pillow is flexible and can be comforted and plumped back to shape after a beating. Those who are basically convinced of their helplessness need to smash cartons. Some stomp on them in rage and tear them apart. Others need to have the carton reinforced with inner cartons to allow them to hit harder and longer. Occasionally a person will pound the floor or wall. Lying on a mattress gives some people a chance to regress to infancy. They express rage by wild kicking, flailing of arms and tossing about.

Some of us have difficulty experiencing anger. Watching others destroy boxes and strangle pillows is therapeutic for us. We need models from whom we can borrow courage.

One young man whose anger had been turned inward against himself for years watched an older man furiously smash half a dozen cartons with deliberate powerful blows like a professional boxer. Later he said to the older man, "It was exciting. It was good to see a strong man express anger that way. I could identify with you and it made me feel manly."

Some of us are verbal types: putting an emotion into words helps us feel it. But some people find that words simply encourage them to intellectualize and move further away from their feelings. Workshop people intuitively discover and teach one another new ways to translate their emotions into concrete actions.

The "push-pull" is a good example. One young woman was tormented by her conflicting attitudes toward me; her self therapy work taught her that her transference on me represented her relationship with her mother. At her suggestion, she and I sat cross-legged on the floor facing one another. She held my shoulders and began to enact her inner conflict: the longing to be close versus the wish for freedom. She held me tight in a loving embrace and then pushed me away, back and forth, back and forth, with increasing intensity of emotion—love and frustration—crying bitterly throughout like a small child. At times she held me rigidly at arm's length, screaming pitifully, "Ma, hold me! Hold me!" while I strained desperately to reach her. There was nothing contrived about this experience. It symbolized a *real life relationship* between the two of us, real live people, not actors in psychodrama. At the same time it represented our own self-defeating life attitudes: her inability to use what I gave; my compulsion to give what cannot be taken.

The "push-pull" has become a workshop tool, used whenever it is truly meaningful. Whenever a student in transference becomes aware of his inner conflict toward me, love versus frustration, dependence versus independence, "come closer" versus "go away," we do the push-pull and he is then able to go deeper into his conflicts toward others, in his private life. Sometimes the push-pull is the conflict between growing into freedom versus the security of staying in the same old neurotic rut. Sometimes it is the adolescent struggle to break away from home. Sometimes the student is shaking me in rage and grief as he would like to shake the parents in his life while he relives old frustrations.

One member used the push-pull to experience in concrete form her ambivalence about intimacy. I sat passively so her hands on my shoulders gave her complete power to hold me close or push me away. Her hands trembled and she discovered that she dared do neither. So intense was the conflict between the *longing for* and the *fear of* closeness that she could only let me stay in the middle distance.

Sometimes a person will request that we play a certain record that has hidden meaning for him and pushes him into self therapy. "Darkness, Darkness" has been useful often to bring one student out of depression into a flood of therapeutic feelings. "I Am a Rock, I Am an Island" helped several to experience their fear and grief about alienation and loneliness.

People learn to pay attention to their bodies. One girl who had difficulty knowing when she was angry, noticed that her arms ached when she needed to hit. She learned to pound a pillow even though she was feeling only a generalized anxiety. In a little while the emotions would bubble up and she could get into gestalt self therapy and come out of it relaxed.

The same student discovered another way of symbolizing a hidden conflict. Once she was lying on the floor in the need of self therpay and she said, "My arms want to push something." She began to push away a nearby footstool. When she indicated she wanted it close by again, another group member pushed it back. Again and again she went through that motion, pushing the piece of furniture away and watching it come back. She seemed surprised, excited and elated, laughing and crying at the same time and her movements were those of a tiny infant. When she finally finished, with an air of satisfaction and triumph she explained that she felt as if she were pushing a wall away. This young woman spent the first three weeks of her life in an incubator. Her fantasy was that she had never before broken out of that box and that now she was beginning to do so.

In another workshop she felt that need in her arms again, began to push away a piece of furniture while another person kept pushing it back. Then she noticed her legs were going through similar motions, so another group member brought a carton over and she then proceeded to go through the motions of pushing something away simultaneously with arms and legs. All this was accompanied by expression of tremendous excitement, deep emotion.

Later she told us, "I felt I was pushing away the walls of the box I live in: the prison walls of my neurosis."

Another time when she went through the process of pushing things away with feet and pulling and pushing with her hands, she came out of it and said it was a variation of the push-pull. She wanted to be free of her neurosis but, fearful of the unknown, she also wanted to stay within the familiar walls.

Watching a man break boxes and tear them apart in rage, a young woman was much shaken. When he was through she continued to show anxiety and said she couldn't stand to see those broken boxes. Crying with an expression of grief and horror, she worked for some time in a vain attempt to put the boxes together again. In a kind of trance she carefully studied the pieces and tried to fit them back where they belonged. When it was over she said her actions had two meanings: trying to keep her hysterical mother from falling apart and trying to bring her broken family together again.

Another device some workshop members have evolved for themselves during self therapy in order to make their experience concrete, is to seek the closeness and darkness of a closet or to cover their heads with a blanket when they were feeling anxiety and fear of people. Some burrow into the arms of a trusted, supportive group member, hiding their heads like frightened little creatures. These actions help them regress to an earlier stage of life and work through old fears.

There is nothing contrived about interaction in my workshops.

We do not use psychodrama or "deliberate regression" [5]. I never suggest that a group member *try* to act like an infant. When he feels that way and wants to sit in someone's lap, his behavior springs from within, from his own therapeutic needs. Nor do I ever suggest that someone act like a parent. Neither I nor any group member is expected to comfort or interact with anyone in a certain way just because of the other person's "needs." Our behavior is spontaneous: we act in accordance with our genuine feelings. If A is crying like a baby and B chooses to rock him in her arms that is because B has a strong desire to do that, B is feeling like a supportive, loving parent at this moment, not because it is "good" for A. Each person is in the workshop for his own personal growth, not merely to "help." The path to growth is authenticity, not acting "as if" he were loving, but following his true feelings.

The result of this reality policy, the avoidance of using group members as props, is that people have a chance to accumulate new and valuable experiences. In self therapy they play through their fantasies, but this interaction with real, live people, sometimes pleasurable, sometimes painful, is in itself therapeutic. Some workshop members never do the work of self therapy, and yet they feel and act healthier after these real life experiences in a therapeutic environment.

Some uptight people, unused to any physical demonstration of affection, are at first uncomfortable and embarrassed at the free-and-easy behavior of others from different backgrounds. Eventually they change and then rejoice in their new-found freedom to accept and give comfort and love in concrete, meaningful terms.

People develop new strengths. A deprived person who regresses to a needy infant soaking up other people's babying, lap-sitting, etc. suddenly shows enormous resources when someone else needs support and comfort. It is exciting to see someone who has been the baby, assume the role of big brother or sister when necessary.

I have learned two facts of life from my workshops: 1) people are flexible and 2) most people, when they feel safe, can care about and love one another. The warmth and trust demonstrated by formerly alienated people, the depth of genuine feelings—rage, jealousy, love, fear, etc.—experienced by those who were once turned-off robots, the courage and honesty displayed by group members who used to appease and manipulate, is a never-ending source of delight and sometimes awe.

I. A SELF THERAPY TECHNIQUE

EACH PERSON has vulnerable areas where, because of his personal history, certain emotions seem too dangerous to feel. Whenever a present situation tempts you to experience that "forbidden" emotion you tend to cover it up with a fake emotion. Each time you hide a feeling from yourself the pseudoemotion tricks you into acting in a self-defeating way; you are not free to use your intelligence and experience to solve the immediate problem.

Self therapy is a tool to peel away the layer of that misleading cover emotion and feel the genuine one just underneath. You need not understand how you got to be this way (you are not your own psychotherapist); just *feel* the hidden emotion and the whole picture will look different to you. When you dare to experience your true feelings, you see people as they really are rather than as shadows from your past, you hear what they are really saying rather than distort and misinterpret. Once you have felt your hidden emotion, you are free to use your experience and intelligence to solve this problem just as you do others in areas where you are not damaged.

Step 1. *Recognize an inappropriate reaction.* You notice yourself reacting to some situation with an emotion your intellect tells you is not appropriate: "Why do I feel so hurt? I know he doesn't mean to hurt me." Since any emotion can be used to cover another, and the fake emotion feels just as real as a genuine, appropriate one, it is difficult to recognize an inappropriate reaction while it is going on, especially if you are a beginner in self therapy. This kind of self-awareness comes more easily with hindsight: "I wonder why I was so angry yesterday. She's only a child!"

Depression, anxiety, obsessive thinking can all be called

inappropriate reactions since they are not definite emotions. They are always covers for something you are afraid to feel. Tension, headache, physical symptoms of anxiety, like breathing difficulty and palpitations, are all clues that you are hiding something from yourself.

Step 2. *Feel the apparent emotion.* Sometimes you deliberately try to avoid an inappropriate reaction ("It's silly to be hurt; he doesn't mean it.") but you must feel that emotion, no matter how irrational it seems. There is no short cut to the unconscious: you cannot feel a hidden emotion unless you begin with the apparent emotion which covers it.

Sometimes the apparent emotion seems dangerous ("I'm so furious I could kill her—but she's only a baby!"). You need not act out your inappropriate feelings: thoughts and actions are not identical, they can be separated. Your feelings have no magic power to do harm. You can always take your apparent emotion somewhere else: you can talk it out, write it out, lock yourself in the bathroom and cry it out. But do not swallow it down.

If you are trying to explore yesterday's inappropriate reaction, warm up that cooled-off emotion by talking about it to a good listener.

Suppose you are tracking down the hidden feeling behind a headache. Be a detective and work backward, looking for clues. When did this symptom begin? What happened then? How did I feel?

Step 3. *What else did I feel?* Just before the apparent feeling, what other feeling did you have? Not a hidden emotion, but one you felt for a brief moment and paid little attention to at the time, one which was drowned out as soon as the apparent emotion was over. You may remember that you felt a pang of fear just before the apparent feeling, anger.

Step 4. *What does this remind me of?* When have you reacted this way to a similar situation? What does this make you think of? Have you ever noticed that you have some peculiar attitudes toward this kind of problem?

If this does not evoke a hidden feeling, ask yourself, *What do I seem to be doing?* For a moment, take an objective view. If you were an outsider, observing your behavior in this situation, what would it *look* as if you were doing?

Here in Step 4 your intellect is asking questions, trying to get a rise out of your emotions. You are not looking for an intellectual explanation for your inappropriate reaction; you are not trying to explain the motives for your self-defeating behavior; you are not your own psychotherapist. You are merely trying to *feel* a hidden emotion. Keep trying different ideas until one of them evokes a new emotion. You will know it is a hidden feeling if it displaces the apparent emotion with which you began.

Step 5. *Look for the pattern.* Do not look for your basic personality pattern at this time, nor anything so broad. Just try to find out what happened here. What hidden emotion were you covering up with what apparent one? You are now predictable to yourself; next time you are faced with a similar problem (tempted to feel that forbidden feeling again), if you can remember what just happened you may not have to cover up again with the same old apparent emotion. You will be free to experiment with a new way of handling the problem; you need not act in the old, automatic, self-defeating way. Now that you know your pattern (the tendency to cover this particular hidden feeling with this apparent feeling under this special set of circumstances), you are free to use your intelligence and experience to act at least as wisely as in those undamaged areas where you never had to hide anything from yourself.

Whenever you look within and dare to feel your true emotion you will be able to hear another's message and know how to respond to it. I had this experience. One evening, when the rattling of pots and pans proclaimed the preparation of supper in the kitchen, my daughter yelled from her room, "When do we eat? I'm *starved!*" Since we always eat at the same hour, the unnecessary question sounded to my harried ears like "What's the matter with the service in this lousy hotel?"

Naturally, I shouted right back, "Stop nagging; act your age; come in and help if you're in such a hurry," etc. This exchange rapidly deteriorated to a hysterical duet. Not until the next day did I recall that we had been going through this off and on for years. Then I reflected (as I had also done for years) that the poor kid couldn't help herself, the "strict" schedule laid down by child guidance experts in her infancy made her cry for her bottle the first few weeks of her life, and here she was, still crying. I understood her problem; I had "analyzed" her unconscious motivation long ago. But it had never helped me to handle her and it did not help now. I could not stand her nagging and I did not know how to shut her up. If you generally get along well with your child as I did, and you find yourself stuck with one special problem over and over again, chances are you are hiding something from yourself. I asked myself, "Why am I handling this situation so awkwardly?" That was Step 1, Notice an inappropriate reaction.

Step 2. Feel the apparent emotion. I was calm now, trying to solve yesterday's problem, so I talked it over with a friend who had a teenager of her own and would be interested and sympathetic. In short order I was re-living yesterday's anger in all its intensity.

Step 3. What else did I feel? Now I could recall that when my daughter first began to yell, just before I became so angry, I felt terribly tense: as if she were standing over me with a whip and I had to hurry, hurry! When the anger came, it released the tension.

Step 4. What does this remind me of; I remembered how she used to cry for the bottle. But that intellectual understanding was not enough, I was still angry ("She's a big girl now. How long must she cry for her bottle?").

What else did this remind me of? Food . . . my compulsive eating; my compulsion to feed my family a balanced diet, etc. Then how did I really feel years ago, when my baby had to cry for her bottle because the pediatrician ordered that I feed her every four hours by the clock?

For the first time I tried deliberately to re-live that scene instead of simply intellectualizing about it. In my mind's eye I saw the baby's room, felt myself standing just outside her door, my eye on my watch, waiting for permission to feed her. I remembered how she cried and how I cried along with her: tears of helplessness, frustration, and . . . guilt. That terrible *guilt* swept over me now in a wave

198

so painful that it felt like yesterday's happening, not years ago. The hidden guilt came out and drowned out all the anger. For fifteen years I had blamed the pediatrician for starving my baby: finally, belatedly, I dared to feel the guilt myself.

Step 5. Look for a pattern. The guilt lasted only a few seconds, and then I could see my pattern. Not the whole design of my relationship with this child, simply the pattern that whenever she screams for food, the old hidden guilt is stirred up and threatens to come out and hurt me. First I tense up and rush around frantically to show what a good mother I am; then, when the tension becomes unbearable, I escape into anger. I act out this self-defeating anger, this pseudoanger, and that encourages her to scream louder. This adds to my hidden guilt which I then cover up with more anger, etc., etc.

Now that I saw my pattern, I was predictable to myself, I could look forward to an opportunity to face this problem again and try to handle it another way. I was not sure yet what I would do next time, but I knew there would be a next time.

Sure enough, about a month later I heard the same old war-cry, "When do we eat? I'm *starved!*" Once again I began to grow tense, but this time, just before the tensions eased into anger, I remembered the hidden guilt. I did not *feel* it again this time: all I did was recall it intellectually. Immediately my tension relaxed and the tone of my child's voice said something quite different to me. Instead of "What's the matter with the service in this lousy hotel?" it sounded more like "Mommy, I'm suffering. Don't you care?"

Of course I cared. Easily, spontaneously, I responded to her hidden message: "Right away, honey. Supper's almost ready." That was all she needed to hear: not another peep out of her.

II. TEN EXAMPLES OF GESTALT SELF THERAPY

THE FOLLOWING are *condensed* versions of actual experiences in gestalt self therapy, five of my own (A to E) and five of my students' (F to J).

A. *The background*

A feeling of resentment, feeling exploited by a student.

Muriel: I'm so tired. What do you want from me?

Student: Help me. Save me. Tell me what to do.

Muriel: You don't want help. You just want me to like you. You don't tell the truth. You lie to me.

Student: Because I'm so scared, so miserable. Muriel, don't you understand? I hate myself and I'm afraid you'll hate me too. That's why I have to lie to you.

Muriel: Oh, poor thing. I do understand. I want to help you, but I can't. I'm so exhausted. (Here I changed the student to Little Muriel.)

Little M: You promised to save me. You promised when you grew up I would be happy. You failed me. I'm still suffering.

Muriel: I'm sorry, I did the best I could. I worked so hard.

Little M: You failed me. Save me. Save me. Take me out of the past. You left me behind.

Muriel: I can't, I can't.

Little Muriel is the neurotic part of me that still reacts

in the same old ways, the part I reach in self therapy that
still suffers the old fears, hurts, frustrations.

B. *The background*

My mother and I, after decades of estrangement, had
established a friendly relationship. During the last years of
her life we saw each other once or twice a year and chatted
on the phone about once a month. I had not seen her for
months, when her husband phoned to tell me she had suddenly
died. Recently I had discovered an old album, pictures as I
remembered her in my first five years before she left me.
Despite my surface courtesy, I had long ago learned to stop
thinking of her as my mother, to distrust her charm and
loving words.

I went to the funeral in a kind of daze, not knowing what I
was feeling. Her body was on display in the open coffin, and
when I looked in I felt a shock of dismay. I did not recognize
my mother. The album snapshots were so fresh in my mind,
the mother of my childhood so much more real than this polite stranger of recent years. I burst into bitter tears: "I
never knew her and now it's too late." I became so obsessed
with this scene that I had to use it for gestalt self therapy
later:

Muriel: (to mother in coffin) You're an impostor. I don't
know you. Where is my mother?

Mother: (in coffin, looks forbidding) I am your mother.
You never knew me. You never loved me. You
were nice to me these last years, you pretended
to love me and I believed you. Now that I'm dead
I know it was all a lie.

Muriel: Forgive me, I didn't know.

Mother: You're cold.

Muriel: Oh, my god, that's what I always said about you.

Mother: You wouldn't let yourself love me.

Muriel: I was afraid to love you. I loved you so much
when I was little and you left me. I didn't want
to be fooled again.

Mother: You had to think, think, think all the time. You had to try to figure me out just the way you keep trying to understand your students. We just want you to love us.
(Here I changed Mother to Student)

Student: Stop trying to be so damned clever. We don't want you to figure us out. We just want you to love us. Don't you understand, you fool? Nobody ever loved us. That's what we need—your heart, not your brain.
(The two sides of Muriel):

Little M: Stop trying so hard, you stupid idiot. Think you're so clever, thinking, thinking all the time. That's not what they need. They need you to be human, real, loving, not a goddamned computer.

Big M: I can't help working hard. It's such a responsibility. I have to understand what's going on. I have to keep trying. I'm sorry. I'll try not to be a computer.

C. *The background*

I received a "poison pen" letter from an old student in whom I had invested years of hard work. He reviled me for my failure to make him feel better, to help him adjust more comfortably to his neurosis. It suddenly became clear to me that I had wasted my time and efforts, that he never had any intention of changing; he belonged to that group of "adjustment" people described in the chapter, "The Inner Conflict". What he mainly wanted from me was pity. I felt anger at his ingratitude and shame at my own stupidity. I began to suffer from obsessive thinking.

Gestalt self therapy

Muriel: You ungrateful thing! I worked so hard and gave you so much and now you write that cruel letter. How could you?

Student: You didn't give me what I wanted. I want! I want! Give me, give me.

EXAMPLES OF GESTALT SELF THERAPY

Muriel: Damn you! What do you want? I'm exhausted from giving to you.

Student: I want pity. Feel sorry for me. I'm starved. Feed me. Give me! Give me!

Muriel: I've been feeding you this nourishing food for years, and all this time you've been spitting it out.

Student: But that's not the food I want. Don't teach me. Just pity me and make me feel better.
(At this point I experienced myself as the food.)

Food: You've been chewing me up all these years. You sucked me dry like an orange and then threw me away. I'm exhausted. I'm an old dried-out orange peel. There's no more juice in me. You sucked it all out.
(Here I changed back to Muriel.)

Muriel: (exhausted, lying on floor) You sucked out the last ounce of pity from me. There's no more left.

D. *The background*

A student, John, accused me of trying to control him, to seduce him into feeling "dangerous" emotions. Although he came to me to learn self therapy, he deliberately fought against letting go, feeling his true emotions. He expressed fear and anger, blaming me for trying to mislead him.

I was hurt and used my old self therapy method to get underneath the apparent emotion. When I asked myself, "What does this remind me of?" I went back to an old student, Dick, who has been stuck in this impasse with his resistance for years, alternately loving and hating me, dependent one week, distrustful and blaming the next. I felt deep pity and concern for his suffering, letting myself recognize that I have no way of knowing which side of Dick will prevail: the fear of changing or the desire to grow. I knew now my feelings about John were the same, and my hurt feelings disappeared.

Next day I started thinking obsessively: endless rehearsal of explaining, arguing, teaching John.

Gestalt self therapy

Muriel: I'm so worried about you. You won't let yourself go, and feel. Why are you so stubborn?

John: I'm afraid to let go. It's dangerous to follow your directions. How do I know you know what's right for me?

Dick: I don't trust you. You're evil.

Muriel: That's not true. I'm a harmless person. I just want to help you.
(Here both John and Dick became one composite student.)

Student: You're so powerful and dangerous. I'm afraid of you.

Muriel: No, no. I'm not. I'm a gentle, loving person.

Student: I don't believe you. You try to manipulate me, to force me to feel against my will. I have to fight you off. I can't give in to you or something bad will happen to me. You want to control me. I won't let you overpower me.

Muriel: I'm not like that. It's not true.

Student: Yes, you are. You're just like your stepmother.
(Here I switched roles. The student became Little Muriel; Muriel became Stepmother.)

Little M: You always try to control me. I'm so afraid of you. Let me live. Let me be myself.

Step-M: (Fierce, threatening.) Do it my way. Obey me. You must do exactly what I say and think, and feel what I want you to. And when you disobey me I'll scare you and break you down. (yelling) I'm big and strong and you're weak and worthless. You're nothing at all.

204

EXAMPLES OF GESTALT SELF THERAPY

Little M: I never let you break me down. I used to dig my fingernails into my hands to distract myself with the pain, so I could keep from showing any feelings.

Step-M: I'll keep yelling until you cry. Show me you're hurt and frightened and humiliated, damn you. Don't stand there like a god-damned statue. I'll break you down yet. I'm stronger than you.

Little M: I turned myself to stone and you can't melt me. It's the only way I can maintain my integrity. I'm too scared to defy you openly, but at least you can't break me down.

But that was so destructive to me. I learned how to stop feeling and made myself so neurotic.

Student: That's how I turn myself off. I have to stop feeling to resist you.

Muriel: I'm sorry I'm such a controlling person. I'll try to change. I'll try to let go, to let you move at your own pace.

Student: I'm suffering. My life is hell. Save me, save me!

Muriel: I don't know how. You don't want me to teach you and I don't know any other way.

Student: Save me, save me! I'm dying.

Muriel: I want to. I'd give anything to save you. I can't. I'm so helpless. What can I do?
(Student becomes Little Muriel)

Little M: Save me, save me! I'm suffering here in the past. Take me out of it.

Muriel: I can't. I want to, but I can't.

Little M: You're abandoning me. Save me, save me.

Muriel: I'm helpless, I can't do it.

(The next day I continued; two sides of myself.)

Topdog: Save them. You must save them.

Under-dog: I try but I can't. I do my best.

(Topdog becomes Stepmother)

Step-M: You're not working hard enough. Come on, work harder.

Muriel: I'm so tired.
(Back to two sides of Muriel)

Topdog: Save them. Save the whole world. Don't stop, that's your job.

Under-dog: I'm tired. I want to let go.

Topdog: Rotten, lazy thing! Don't you dare rest. Work! Save them all.

Under-dog: Oh, please let me rest. I'm exhausted. (Lying on floor) I feel so helpless. Stop driving me. Get off my back, damn you. I hate you. You're crazy. You're trying to kill me. Let me live.

Little by little I am letting go, giving my students more freedom to move at their own pace, giving myself more freedom to rest and have fun

E. *The background*

One of my students indulged in a temper tantrum and acted in a cruel, degrading way to another. I felt so punishing and judgmental about this that I did not trust myself to speak to him until I worked it through.

Gestalt self therapy

Muriel: You cruel, heartless thing! How could you say dreadful things. You're not human.

Student: Hah, hah! (threatening with claw-like gestures of hands, distorted face) I'll claw you, I'll tear you to pieces.

206

EXAMPLES OF GESTALT SELF THERAPY

Muriel: You're just like Mrs. L (sadistic foster mother I lived with, age 7 to 9 years).

Mrs. L: I'm a witch and I'll scare you to death. You're at my mercy. You can't escape. (whipping Muriel) I hate you and I'll beat you down.

Little M: (crying) Please, don't whip me. I'm so scared. Have mercy!

Mrs. L: Mercy? Hah, hah! On your knees, little worm.

Student: I'd like to whip people, but I just cut them down with words.

Muriel: Like S (stepmother with whom I spent my adolescence).

Step-M: (sneering) Muriel, you're worthless. Nothing you do is any good. I'll degrade you and humiliate you until you can't lift your head.

Muriel: I'm so afraid of your cruel tongue.

Step-M: You'd better be afraid. I'll cut you to ribbons with my clever tongue. You can't defend yourself against me.

Muriel: Oh my God, that's me. That's how I feel about this student. (hitting student) You rotten thing! How dare you act that way! I'll beat you down, I'll punish you. I'll degrade you. I'll make you hate yourself.

Student: Please don't do that. I hate myself enough already. I can't take any more. Have mercy.
(Here I switched to the two sides of Muriel: Tough and Gentle.)

Gentle M: I'm afraid of you. I never knew you were part of me. You're just like S and Mrs. L, you monster!

Tough M: (sneering) Oh, sweet little saintly Muriel. You rotten phony, pretending you're so perfect. Never get angry, never feel judgmental, oh no! Just keeping me underground all the time.

Gentle M: I don't want to be cruel or punishing. I don't want any part of you.

Tough M: Well, here I am. I am punishing and judgmental and I get angry. I'm sick of your weakness and phoniness. (screaming, hitting Gentle Muriel) Cut it out. Stop acting so damn saintly. Stop being such a phony. I hate you. I hate you, you big fake.

Gentle M: (crying) I'm afraid of you. You'll devastate my students. They're so vulnerable they can't stand rejection or punishment. You'll kill them. I can't let you near them.

After this I became keenly aware of neurotic symptoms—headache, obsessive thinking—when hiding that "cruel" side of me, over-compensating (for fear of being like my step-mother, S and my foster mother, Mrs. L) by too much gentleness. I have gone back to this conflict often, exploring other problems. More and more as I face the fear of being cruel, I have less need to hide it with unnatural sweetness. My students observe a new toughness which they experience as strength and sincerity and it is more reassuring to them than the old softness.

Another time, exploring a similar situation, one student being cruel to another, in gestalt self therapy:

Victim: Muriel save me from her. I'm so afraid of her. I'm so helpless and she's so powerful and cruel. (Victim becomes Little Muriel)

Little M: Save me from Mrs. L. I'm so afraid and little and alone.

Big M: I wish I could turn back the clock and save you. I can't, I can't.

F. *The background*

In communication workshop Frieda was told her seven-year-old, Jamie, was too difficult for some people to handle. He kicked them, destroyed their property, and since Frieda

EXAMPLES OF GESTALT SELF THERAPY

would not let anyone lay a hand on him, they were powerless to protect themselves and were beginning to feel hostile toward Jamie. Frieda could not accept their right to handle Jamie themselves with any show of force.

Gestalt self therapy

Frieda: Oh, Jamie, my smallest child! You're such a little, little boy and things have been so rough in the family since you were born. I'll take care of you. I'll protect you. I won't let anyone hurt you.

Jamie: I know. Hardly anything I do bothers you.

Frieda: That's right, my child. I wish you would be nice so people would like you, but I can't get angry with you, I can't let them hurt you. You're so little and I know you try to be good. I'll protect you. You're such a tiny thing, like me, and you're the only one of my children who looks like me.
(Here she switches roles. Frieda becomes her grandma, who brought her up, and Jamie becomes Little Frieda.)

Grand-ma: I'll take care of you, my child. Don't worry about anything.

Little F: But why don't my daddy and mommy live together? Why doesn't my daddy live here?

Grand-ma: Never mind, my child. Don't bother your head about such things. Your daddy loves you.

Little F: How do you know he loves me? Did he tell you?

Grand-ma: I know, I know. No, he didn't tell me in those words, but I can tell.

Little F: Then why won't he live with me? And why is Mommy so mean?

Grand-ma: You're too young to understand. You don't have to think about such things. Don't listen and don't

209

see anything bad. Be happy. A little girl should be happy. I'll protect you. I won't let anything bad happen to you. I love you.

Little F: I know you love me, but you protected me so well I grew up without knowing anything about the real world, and now look at the trouble I'm in. (Back to Frieda and Jamie)

Frieda: Oh Jamie, I love you so much I'm protecting you from knowing the real world. You're being bad to people and they can't love you and you don't understand. You don't know the only reason they don't hit you is because of me. I'm not being fair to you. You're getting a crazy picture of the world, just like me.

Frieda came out of this experience with a determination to somehow modify her attitude toward her adult friends and their behavior toward Jamie; to give him a chance to know reality.

G. *The background*

Miriam's "friendship" with Ella was a transference relationship in which she felt emotionally dependent on Ella. Miriam's obsessive thinking swung back and forth from intense affection and equally intense resentment against what seemed like Ella's manipulation and teasing.

Gestalt self therapy

Miriam: I'm sick and tired of feeling like this. I want to stop thinking about you. I don't want to have to see you so often. You're driving me crazy.

Ella: I don't know what you mean. I haven't done anything. Come here. Go away.

Miriam: That double-talk of yours, those confused messages are getting me all mixed up. Stop teasing me.

Ella: (swings an imaginary string back and forth) Here

kitty, kitty, kitty! Catch this. Come on, try to catch it. Hah, hah! I won't let you.

Miriam: (on the floor in attitude of kitten, head swinging desperately back and forth, trying to catch imaginary object swinging before her eyes) Damn you, cut it out! Stop teasing me. Stop it, I say. Leave me alone. Just like my mother.

Mother: Miriam dear, do it my way. I understand you perfectly. Just listen to me. Do this, do that, come on, I'll tell you what to do.

Miriam: Leave me alone. LEAVE ME ALONE, damn it. Get off my back. Let me live my own life. Let me think my own thoughts.
(Here she switched to two sides of herself.)

Topdog: Come on now, work hard. Get perfect grades in school. Always be polite and appease people, tell them what they want to hear. Entertain them with jokes. Don't indulge yourself. Don't have any fun. Don't show any feelings. Keep your cool at all times.

Under- Get off my back. I'm sick of you. Stop ruining
dog: my life. Let me live. Leave me alone! LEAVE ME ALONE! damn you.

After this, Miriam began to wean herself away from her painful dependency on Ella, using gestalt and other self therapy techniques whenever she was aware of acting out her irrational cravings. She also began in small ways to modify her perfectionist pattern, experimenting with small doses of anxiety. As she allowed herself more spontaneity, people began to notice that her face became more expressive and attractive, that she was losing a former rigidity and appearance of coldness.

H. *The background*

Sylvia depended on her husband to make decisions for the family's welfare. She acted as if she was incapable of assuming responsibility, waited passively in the hope that he would make wise decisions, complained bitterly and suffered helplessness and anxiety on those occasions when she thought he failed.

Gestalt self therapy

Sylvia: Take care of us. Be responsible. Everything in the family is your responsibility. I can't make these important decisions. Why don't you? Why do you make wrong decisions? It's terrible when you make mistakes. I worry so about the children's welfare and I can't do anything. I'm so helpless. Do it! Do it right! Make things right! I'm so scared. I feel like a helpless child.
(Goes back to childhood)

Little S: Daddy, take care of Momma. Be good to her. She's suffering and I can't take care of her.

ıma: Sylvia, take care of me. I'm dying. Find your Daddy. Make him come home. I'm dying, save me, save me.

Little S: I can't, I can't. I want to but I'm only a little girl. I tried so hard to save you, to fix things up with you and Daddy, but I can't. Daddy, please take care of Momma. I can't stand to see her suffer and I'm only a little girl. I can't do it.
(here she comes back to her present self)

Sylvia: I want to save the world. I can't stand all the suffering. I want to make them all happy.

World: Save us, save us. We're suffering. Look at the injustice, the cruelty, the deprivation. Change it.

Sylvia: I've been trying all my life, but I can't do it.
(two sides of Sylvia)

Topdog: You are responsible for everybody. Try harder. Be smarter. Study more. Work harder. Don't rest.

Under-dog: I can't do it. I'm so exhausted. (Lying down) I just want to rest. I can't carry that burden any

more. So tired, so tired. Just want to lie here
and rest, not move.

After this, Sylvia began to assume more responsibility in
the family. At times when her attitude differed sharply from
her husband's, she was able to assert herself and stand by
her convictions. With continued self therapy she also began
to be more realistic about her limitations in saving the
world, with less tendency to rush into impulsive, self-
defeating action.

I. *The background*

During a gestalt self therapy workshop, I cried hard while
exploring a problem of my own, acting as a model for the
group. When I finished, Sylvia began to work.

Gestalt self therapy

Sylvia: Oh, Muriel, I can't stand to see you cry. It tears
me up. Can't stand to see you suffer. I want to
say, stop it. Stop suffering. I know this reminds
me of my mother. Momma, stop crying. Please
stop. I can't stand it.

Mother: (crying) Sylvia, I'm dying. Save me. Take care
of me. Tell Poppa to come home. Oh, Sylvia,
I'm so unhappy. I'm dying.

Sylvia: Stop it, Momma. I can't stand to hear you.
You're disgusting. You repel me—ugh! Can't
stand that weakness.
(changes to Strong Sylvia and Weak Sylvia)

Strong S: I can't stand your weakness. You repel me, disgust me—ecch! You make me sick.

Weak S: (crying) I'm so weak and helpless. I can't help
it. I want to be strong, but I can't. I'm just like
Momma.

Sylvia: Oh, poor Momma. Poor little thing. You can't
help it. Poor helpless little thing. (crying) I'm
sorry Momma. (cradles Momma in her arms) I

213

love you, poor little thing. I'm sorry you're suffering. I wish I could help you.

This acceptance of her mother's weakness was new for Sylvia and indicated that the gap between her strong and weak sides was narrowing. She now finds herself more open to her true feelings, more capable of experiencing and showing hurt instead of using an old system: covering it up with fake anger.

J. *The background*

Agnes came to a workshop and announced that she didn't feel like working.

Gestalt self therapy

Agnes: I just don't feel like doing the work here. I don't feel like doing anything I'm supposed to do. I'm tired of always being so damned good. I want to quit my job and stop doing all the "nice" things I've done all my life. I'm tired of being the perfect hostess. I could have kicked myself after I offered my home for the last workshop party. I was irritable all week and had a perfectly miserable time at that party. I've never been this way before. I can't imagine what's come over me.

Mother: (in a prissy, indignant voice) I can't imagine what's come over you. Why, you *have* to be hospitable. That's the way we do things in our family. Now you behave yourself and do things properly. I just don't know what you think you're talking about. I don't want to hear any more of that. That's enough!

Agnes: (boldly) Well, that's where I am now. I'm sick of doing things your way. I don't want to be your good little girl any more. The hell with that! I'm going to do things my way from now on and if you don't like it you can lump it.

EXAMPLES OF GESTALT SELF THERAPY

Mother: Now that's enough of that. You'll just have to behave yourself. No more nonsense.

Agnes: I won't obey you any more. I'm a big girl now. (begins to tremble.) I don't know why I'm shaking like this. I guess I'm scared, but I don't know what I'm afraid of. (Keeps quiet for a while and lets herself shake. The shaking grows more violent. Goes back to the mother of her childhood.)

Mother: (fiercely) How dare you talk that way! You think you can disobey me? I'll show you, I'll teach you! (whips Agnes)

Agnes: (crying) Oh, please don't! I'll be good. I want to be good but I can never please you. Why do you spank me all the time, no matter what I do? Why would you want to hit a little girl?

Mother: (calmly hitting) That's the only way to bring up a child. How would you know how to behave if I didn't spank you regularly. I have to do it.

Agnes: Somebody help me, save me! Daddy, please help me. Mother spanks me all the time and I'm so afraid of her. You don't know. You're not here when she does it. Please protect me.

Daddy: I don't know what you mean Agnes. How can I help you. I have things to do. You'll have to excuse me now.

Agnes: (screams) What kind of a father are you? What kind of a man are you? Don't you give a damn about me? I'm your little girl and I'm so scared. (Agnes is still shaking. She lies down on the floor.)

Agnes: (crying) I'm a little, little girl and I'm lying here on the living room floor crying, hoping someone will hear me and care. I'm so cold here in my nightie. Won't anyone come and comfort me? Doesn't anyone care? Please Daddy or Mother

215

come and put your hand on my cheek and tell me
you love me. (sobbing loudly) Just once tell me
you love me. If I could just hear it once it would
last me a long time. Nobody hears, nobody
cares. It's so cold here. I guess I'd better get
up and go back to my bed.

Big A: Get up Agnes. No point waiting for them. Just
take care of yourself. Stop all that crying. It
won't get you anywhere.

Little A: But I wish they would comfort me.

Big. A: Well, they won't, so snap out of it.

Agnes: The shaking stopped. I don't feel scared any
more. Funny, I was so brave and rebellious. I
didn't know I was scared underneath. I guess I
have to change a little at a time, but I don't want
to be her good little girl any more. Boy, I'd like
to shock her. (laughs out loud) I know what I'd
like to do! Go back to that small, gossipy town
and walk naked down main street. That would
give my mother something to think about. She'd
hang her head down for the rest of her life.

NOTE: All examples of gestalt self therapy in this book are
condensed. I have indicated change in role and mood but not
the length of time required for each stage.

III. COMMUNICATION WORKSHOPS

(Excerpts from an article by James Elliott in THE GROUP LEADER'S WORKSHOP/GROUPS & ORGANIZATIONS, copyright 1968, Explorations Institute.)

"Self Therapy," Muriel Schiffman told us, "is a system where you notice yourself reacting to something in an irrational way. Maybe your intellect says to you, 'Gee, that's funny; how come I'm so angry?' And then—and I'm over-simplifying—you say to yourself, 'Hmm, what does that remind me of?' 'Well, my God, it reminds me of what my father used to do when he cut me down!' And then some other feeling crops up. 'How did I feel then? I was terribly hurt. I felt so rejected.' And then you feel the actual rejection, which lasts only a couple of seconds, and the apparent feeling with which you began, the anger, is gone. And then you're able to look at this person in a slightly different light. You realize he's not really your father, he's talking out of his own experience. And instead of hitting him with that fake anger, you're able to say, 'God, that hurt!' And he is able to say, 'I didn't know. I didn't mean to hurt you.' Whereas, if you had responded from the apparent feeling—'Damn you!'— then he has to hit *you* harder, and this can go on forever."

- - - - -

Results of the weekend groups, Muriel said, are fabulous. "People with whom I worked for years, in one or two weekends, it was like they were wide open. It was just amazing. I'd get calls. Like the man who called and said, 'My God, I don't know what you did to my wife, but for the first time in twelve years of marriage, she's affectionate! She's able to kiss her children, whom she could never lay a hand on.' Or like the woman who called and said, 'I don't know what you did to my husband, but he's changed toward his children. He's so accepting. He says, ''Well, if you're going to smoke, you'd better smoke in the house.'' ' Fabulous!''

The main difference between the weekend and the once-a-week groups is that in the weekend group, participants become, for a while, a part of Muriel's family . . . "It's a family in many ways. For one thing, I'm indulging a need of mine to feed people. I'm a Jewish mother, and this is apparently terribly important to me. I had no idea what gratification I would get from this. They love the food, and what they tell me is they love the fact that I'm coaxing them to eat. And that I obviously get pleasure when they're hungry. And when they're not, I worry. Like, people sometimes get upset stomachs from their emotions—they can't eat—and I feed them yogurt, and this they love. Apparently for those that didn't have a Jewish mother, this is very meaningful. And the home is theirs. They can go to the fridge and scrounge around. It's their house. They can go into one of the bedrooms and take a nap.''

- - - - -

"I'm basically a product of my own ethnic background,'' explained Muriel, "very demonstrative, volatile. And people would flinch and be frightened, so I had learned to be cautious and careful. But in these weekends, I don't care. I do whatever I feel like doing, and if they flinch, well, we talk about that. 'Did it bother you when I did that?' And they'll say, 'No, I loved it, but I'm so embarrassed, I don't know how to respond to it,' '' However, she adds, "I may want to hug a person, but if I'm pretty sure that this is a person who'll stop crying if he's comforted, then I won't. I won't touch him; I'll let him cry. But other people may be crying in such a choked way that if I hold them tight and I say, 'Okay, let go,' *then* they can start to sob, then it comes out.''

"One way to break down people's defenses,'' she went on, "is the attack method; you know, in the Synanon square games. Well, apparently, love is even more powerful, because these people are wide open. It's just incredible. They'll talk about things they never thought they would share with anybody, and they will cry about things they've been intellectualizing about for decades.

"The theory of my workshop is that I am presenting a model family. This is the way family life could be if we dare to be honest with one another. And my family presents a model. Bernie and I are our natural selves. I do a lot of crying; I cry at least once in every weekend."

Both Muriel's daughters, now in their early twenties, have been members of her weekend groups. "Now, what the kids did when they were here was to work on old problems that never dared come out in the open before. One time it was a very painful encounter between my younger daughter and her father; another time, my older daughter and me. Each time, something important happened with us, and this was a terrific thing for the group: to learn that a real live family can talk openly about their feelings, and the other person can *listen*. And everybody gets in on the act. This is encouraged. You're encouraged to say, 'I feel protective of the victim,' 'I feel angry at the aggressor,' 'You don't understand!' If you have any feeling about what happens, you're supposed to say it, so generally there's a scrap between either of us— Bernie or me—and a child, or any of the young people and any of the adults. There's always a struggle between generations, and whenever this happens, the group gets split down the middle, with half the people identifying with the child and half with the parent. And everybody gets in and tries to explain and argues and scolds, and they do whatever they have to do, and then the amazing thing to me, and this never happened in the old groups, is right then and there, people do self therapy. Someone will burst into tears: 'Oh, my goodness, he's just like my father; he never could hear me, just the way you can't hear her.' And somebody else will say, 'Oh, my God, I never heard my son. I realize now he's been trying and trying to get through to me.' The struggle goes on, and by Sunday night, the kids are saying, 'Oh, I'm so grateful to you that you're able to hear me. Maybe my father will hear me, maybe I can try again.' Or: 'If only my father could.' And the adults are saying, 'Oh, you give me so much hope, maybe my daughter will believe that I love her if I tell her.' First they cry about the chances they missed, and then they feel some hope.

"The main thing that I see that's different here from any of the once-a-week groups is the tremendous amount of love. And I'm evolving a new theory. We've always been taught that the main problem of our culture is the suppressed and repressed hostility. And we have to have all these attack encounter groups to encourage people to express their hostility. Well, I'm discovering that—as far as my people are concerned, and they're really a cross-section of society—the main thing I notice is that people are afraid to feel loving, to accept love, to feel love, to express love. People I've known for years in the other groups are so affectionate here, it's just amazing.

"The format of the weekend workshop is that it's as much like real life as possible. No let's-all-hold-hands, no psychodrama. It's like real life in the sense that nobody is here to help you, we are all here just to hear what you're saying and tell you what you're doing to us. We are not your therapists. We're not here to do anything for you; we're here only to speak the truth as if we were in the same family: 'You're hurting me,' 'You're frightening me.' I'm teaching them to say, 'I have a terrible need to reassure you,' rather than *trying* to reassure. 'I would *love* to help you, but I feel so helpless, I don't know how.' They *do* act helpful, they *do* act reassuring, and time and again somebody will point out how non-helpful they're being, how non-reassuring they're being. So then I say, 'Why don't you try, in this group, just to talk about how you feel instead of doing it.' And they are learning that it's possible to do this at home; they find they're getting places much faster by just talking about their feelings rather than trying to do something.

"I've had several young people who have been in lots and lots of T-groups and confrontation groups, and their first complaint is, 'What's going on here? There's not enough going on. Not enough interaction. How come you started a scrap and you stopped in the middle? I'm so disappointed. Come on, finish it up!' When people reach an impasse, they have the illusion that if they only fight harder, they'll work it out. And so their first reaction Friday night and Saturday is frustration. 'Everything is all wrong here. This is crazy. And boring.' By Sunday, they're just awed. They can't *believe* what's happening. Because they discover that just a scrap doesn't necessarily resolve anything if the people who are acting angry are just covering up something else. If you're pretending to be strong, to cover weakness, then it can go on forever, and there is no resolution. So then they see that people are daring, in this particular situation, where they're so safe, to stop in midstream, with a little help from me.

"For instance, a man can be sounding off and lecturing and scolding the kids and cutting them down, and they're furious, all up in arms, ready to kill him, you know. And at one point this man who was acting so strong and domineering said something about feeling kind of anxious—just a little throwaway line—and I knew him from other groups, and I seized on that. I said, 'Stay with the anxiety; tell us about that.' And *then* it was able to come out—that all this blustering was just a cover, because he was so unsure of himself and his *own* values that he had to pretend he was sure so his children wouldn't know how unsure he was, and that's why he was so powerful. And then he was able to cry. And then things just changed. The whole thing changed.

"I think this can only happen because the people feel so safe. They feel so loved that they dare to face things about themselves that they never faced, and they dare to share with their peers."

The four evening groups which Muriel formerly led continued to meet during the summer of 1968, while she experimented with the concentrated weekend workshops, then reorganized themselves into three groups which are now continuing without leaders. These autonomous groups accept people who have been through the weekend workshops, with occasional advice from Muriel with regard to some applicants.

REFERENCES

1. THE GREAT SHORT STORIES OF ROBERT LOUIS STEVENSON, The Pocket Library

2. GOOD AND EVIL, Martin Buber, The Scribner Library

3. GESTALT THERAPY VERBATIM, Frederick Perls, Real People Press

4. SELF THERAPY Techniques for Personal Growth, Muriel Schiffman, Self Therapy Press

5. TRANSACTIONAL ANALYSIS IN PSYCHOTHERAPY, Eric Berne, Evergreen Press

6. NEUROSIS AND TREATMENT, Andras Angyal, Wiley and Sons

7. lectures by Virginia Satir, author of CONJOINT FAMILY THERAPY, Science & Behavior

8. THE FAMILY NEUROSIS, Grotjahn

9. TOWARD A PSYCHOLOGY OF BEING, Abraham Maslow

10. THE PSYCHOPATH, McCord and McCord, Van Nostrand Co.

11. THE ADJUSTED AMERICAN, Putney

12. CLINICAL STUDIES IN PSYCHIATRY, Harry Stack Sullivan, Norton & Co.

13. REMEMBRANCE OF THINGS PAST, Marcel Proust, book I: SWANN

14. LONELINESS, Clark E. Moustakas, Prentice-Hall

15. THE LONELY CROWD, David Riesman

16. JEAN CHRISTOPHE, Romain Rolland

17. LOOK HOMEWARD ANGEL, Thomas Wolfe

REFERENCES

18. A WALKER IN THE CITY, Alfred Kazan

19. I NEVER PROMISED YOU A ROSE GARDEN, Hannah Greene

20. CREATIVITY AND CONFORMITY, Clark E. Moustakas

21. THE INFORMED HEART, Bruno Bettelheim

22. MARTIN LUTHER, Erik Erikson

23. CHILDHOOD AND SOCIETY, Erik Erikson, Norton & Co.

24. THE VANISHING ADOLESCENT, Friedenberg

25. GROWING UP ABSURD, Paul Goodman

26. THE PSYCHOLOGY OF WOMEN, Helena Deutsch

27. MAN THE MANIPULATOR, Everett Shostrum

28. THE SANE SOCIETY, Erich Fromm

29. DEVELOPMENT OF NEUROSIS, David Ausubel

30. IT'S HAPPENING, Simmons and Winograd

31. ALL MY CHILDREN, Jacqui Lee Schiff, Evans and Co.

32. SO FAIR A HOUSE, THE STORY OF SYNANON, Caserel; THE TUNNEL BACK, Yablonsky

33. AN ANALYSIS OF THE KINSEY REPORTS, Geddes

34. AN OUTLINE OF PSYCHOANALYSIS, edited by Thompson, Mazer and Witenberg, Modern Library, Random House, 1955